CULTURAL AND ENVIRONMENTAL HISTORY OF CIENEGA VALLEY SOUTHEASTERN ARIZONA

ANTHROPOLOGICAL PAPERS OF
THE UNIVERSITY OF ARIZONA
NUMBER 43

CULTURAL AND ENVIRONMENTAL HISTORY OF CIENEGA VALLEY SOUTHEASTERN ARIZONA

Frank W. Eddy
Maurice E. Cooley
with sections by
Paul S. Martin
Bruce B. Huckell

THE UNIVERSITY OF ARIZONA PRESS
TUCSON, ARIZONA
1983

About the authors...

FRANK W. EDDY has focused his professional career on research concerning human adaptation and cultural ecology. He has directed and been involved with large scale site survey projects and excavations located in Arizona, New Mexico, Utah, Texas, Colorado, Virginia, and Egypt, and he has authored and coauthored numerous monographs and articles on these field programs. Eddy received degrees in anthropology from the University of New Mexico (B.A., 1952), the University of Arizona (M.A., 1958), and the University of Colorado (Ph.D., 1968). In various capacities he has been employed by the U.S. National Park Service; the universities of Utah, Arizona, and Texas at Austin; and the Museum of New Mexico. He joined the faculty of the University of Colorado-Boulder in 1970, where he became an Associate Professor in 1974.

MAURICE E. COOLEY received a Bachelor of Arts degree from the University of Colorado in 1950, and a Master of Science degree in geology from the University of Arizona in 1957. Since then he has been employed by the U.S. Geological Survey, first with the Arizona Water Resources Division in Tucson, and subsequently with the Water Resources Division in Cheyenne, Wyoming. Throughout his professional career, Cooley has been involved in research dealing with various aspects of ground water and aquifers and with environmental reconstruction of the geological past, including both bedrock geology and unconsolidated Quaternary sediments.

THE UNIVERSITY OF ARIZONA PRESS

Copyright © 1983
The Arizona Board of Regents
All Rights Reserved

This book was set in 10/11 V-I-P Times Roman
Manufactured in the U.S.A.

Library of Congress Cataloging in Publication Data

Eddy, Frank W.
    Cultural and environmental history of Cienega Valley, southeastern Arizona.
      (Anthropological papers of the University of Arizona; no. 43)

    Includes bibliographical references and index.
    1. Indians of North America—Arizona—Cienega Creek Valley
Antiquities. 2. Cienega Creek Valley (Ariz.)—Antiquities.
3. Arizona—Antiquities. I. Cooley, M. E. (Maurice E.) II. Title. III. Series.
E78.A7E32 1983   979.1'53   83-17942

ISBN 0-8165-0830-5

CONTENTS

FOREWORD	vii
Emil W. Haury	
PREFACE	ix
1. CIENEGA VALLEY	1
Present Environment	1
Physiography	1
Climate	2
Vegetation	4
Paul S. Martin	
Wildlife	5
Environmental Conditions of the Historic Past	6
Geological Stratigraphy	6
Cretaceous Rocks	6
Pleistocene Deposits	6
Late Recent Alluvium	7
Unit 7	7
Unit 6	8
Unit 5	8
Unit 4	8
Unit 3	9
Unit 2, Sanford formation	9
Unit 1	9
2. CULTURAL SEQUENCE	10
Archaeological Sites	10
Preceramic Sites	10
Arizona EE:2:12	10
Arizona EE:2:30	10
Arizona EE:2:35	10
Ceramic Sites	10
Buried Pit Houses	10
Buried Trash Zones	11
Sheet Erosion Sites	12
Ridge Sites	15
Buried Historic Remains	15
Cochise Culture	17
San Pedro Stage	17
Excavations	17
Artifacts	18
Ground stone	18
Chipped stone	21
Bone	22
Burials	22
Discussion	23
Hohokam Culture	23
Vahki-Estrella Phase	23
Snaketown Phase	24
Cañada del Oro Phase	25
Undifferentiated Cañada del Oro-Rillito Phase	25
Rincon Phase	26
Tanque Verde Phase	27
Tucson Phase	27
Discussion of the Cultural Sequence	27
3. GEOCHRONOLOGY AND DATING	31
Radiocarbon Dating	31
Ceramic Dating	32
Historical Dating	33
Age of the Alluvial Units	33
Rates of Alluviation	35
4. PAST ENVIRONMENTS	37
Late Recent Environmental Fluctuations	37
Drainage Pattern and Environment of Units 3 and 4	40
Pollen Profile from the East Bank of Cienega Creek	42
Paul S. Martin	
Wood Identification	44
Freshwater and Land Invertebrates	44
Mammals	44
Comparison of Data Used in Environmental Interpretation	44
5. CULTURAL AND ENVIRONMENTAL HISTORY	46
Early San Pedro Stage	46
Late San Pedro Stage and Early Pioneer Period	47
Late Pioneer Period	47
Colonial and Sedentary Periods	47
Classic Period	47
Discussion	50
Appendix A: Stratigraphic Section MC–5	51
Appendix B: Stratigraphic Section MC–6	53
Appendix C: Additional Chronological Data on Cienega Valley, Arizona	57
Bruce B. Huckell	
References	59
Index	61

FIGURES

1.1. Cienega Creek Basin, southeastern Arizona — 2

1.2. Cienega Valley: area of confluence of Matty Wash and Cienega Creek — 3

1.3. Cienega Valley: drainage patterns, physiographic features, archaeological sites, and stratigraphic sections — 3

1.4. Diagrammatic profile of Empire Valley vegetation — 5

1.5. West bank of Cienega Creek at Section MC–6 — 7

1.6. Schematic cross section of Cienega Valley, illustrating the intertonguing relationships between sediments and archaeological sites — 8

2.1. Stone tools from preceramic surveyed sites — 11

2.2. Matty Wash at Arizona EE:2:30 — 12

2.3. West bank of Matty Wash at Test 1, Arizona EE:2:30 — 13

2.4. Test 3, Arizona EE:2:30 — 13

2.5. East bank of Cienega Creek above the lower falls at Arizona EE:2:35 — 14

2.6. Cooking Pit 4 after excavation at Arizona EE:2:35 — 14

2.7. Early Pioneer period pit house exposed in the east bank of Matty Wash at Arizona EE:2:10 — 16

2.8. Colonial period pit house in the east bank of Matty Wash at Arizona EE:2:34 — 16

2.9. Plan and section of superimposed pits at Arizona EE:2:30 — 18

2.10. Handstones from Arizona EE:2:30 — 19

2.11. Ground stone tools from Arizona EE:2:30 — 19

2.12. Chipped and ground stone tools from Arizona EE:2:30 — 20

2.13. Bone tools from Arizona EE:2:30 — 22

2.14. Pit house excavated at Arizona EE:2:34 — 25

2.15. Rincon phase ceramic vessels — 26

2.16. Correlation of the geological events, cultural sequences, pollen record, and radiocarbon dates in Cienega Valley — 28

3.1. Age range of Unit 3 sediments in the Cienega Valley — 34

4.1. Cienega Valley: late Recent environmental conditions and distribution of sites — 38

4.2. Annual precipitation plots from stations in southeastern Arizona showing the drought of 1892 to 1904 — 41

4.3. Pollen profile from Cienega Creek near Section MC-6 — 43

5.1. Isometric fence diagram of Cienega Valley, Arizona, illustrating Recent alluvial stratigraphic relationships — 48

TABLES

1.1. Climatic data from stations near the Empire Valley — 4

1.2. Dominant range grasses in the Empire Valley — 5

2.1. Identification of charcoal and beams from archaeological sites in Cienega Valley — 15

2.2. Mammal bones from Arizona EE:2:30 — 17

2.3. San Pedro stage stone tool complexes from the study area compared with complexes from adjacent regions — 19

2.4. Occurrence of ceramics on sites within Cienega Valley — 24

3.1. Radiocarbon dates for Cienega Valley — 31

3.2. Rates of deposition of the Recent alluvium in Cienega Valley — 35

4.1. Freshwater and land invertebrates from Recent alluvial units in Cienega Valley — 44

C.1. Cienega Valley radiocarbon dates by the gas method — 57

C.2. Calibrated radiocarbon dates from the Cienega Valley area — 58

FOREWORD

Much of the work of archaeologists is centered on demolished buildings and their surroundings. Although nature and sometimes man have been unkind to them, they stand as the visible achievements of another people in another time.

The discovery of finely chipped stone projectile points lying next to bones of extinct bison at Folsom, New Mexico, in 1926, and the presence of grinding stones with bones of fossil animals, notably mammoth, camel, and horse, in the alluvial deposits dissected by Whitewater Draw in southeastern Arizona at about the same time, opened new doors and challenges for the archaeologist. In both of these instances, the valuable evidences of human activity were deeply buried, masked under a heavy blanket of soil deposited by nature that left no hints of them on the surface of the ground. Through arroyo cutting, nature, as the master excavator, exposed these long-buried vestiges to the probing eyes of the curious.

Evidences such as these confront the archaeologist with new problems. Clearly the context in which the material occurs is geological. An explanation calls for the skills of the earth scientist. The identification of the associated bones of long-dead animals requires the help of the paleontologist. Further, because the succession of geological beds and the contained biological remains, whether plant or animal, are indicators of past climates, the knowledge of the climatologist must be depended on to reach an understanding of environmental characteristics of the time represented. Immediately the interpretation of the human traces demands the expert help from other disciplines. The archaeologist's role is reduced to understanding the artifacts left behind, the human behavior they indicate, and man's responses to his physical setting.

Given this cooperative effort, our knowledge of human occupation in the Southwest has been vastly enriched in the last half century and, most importantly, has pushed back the accepted time of man's appearance far beyond the age of the impressive surface ruins, dating to the last millennium or two, to at least 11,000 years ago. What we know of the Paleo-Indians, the first people here, and the Archaic tradition of subsequent times has grown out of this kind of archaeological probing.

For those of us fascinated by what can be seen in the banks of arroyos, as at Folsom and in Whitewater Draw, gully-walking has come to be an absorbing and productive activity. The kill sites where hunters successfully brought their big prey to earth and butchered it, and the camp sites where they tarried, signaled by concentrations of artifacts and in-place hearths, have been found in this way. The Clovis and Folsom hunters and the Cochise foragers have emerged.

The Cochise culture brings us immediately to the point of this monograph. Ted Sayles and Ernst Antevs, building on the initial discovery by Byron Cummings at the Double Adobe site in Whitewater Draw, recognized three stages, called Sulphur Spring, Chiricahua, and San Pedro, ranging in time from about 8000 B.C. to A.D. 1, each stage characterized by certain artifacts and environmental conditions. This report is significant because it deals with the latest stage, the San Pedro, radiocarbon dated to the first millennium before and to the time of Christ. Physically, the deposits under study were buried by deep alluvium in the inner valley of Cienega Creek and a principal tributary, Matty Wash.

The in situ evidence of San Pedro materials consisted of hearths, pits, and use-surfaces. These, together with the artifacts in the cultural matrix, can be accepted as "pure" or unmixed with earlier materials. Furthermore, the depth of the overlying sediments of several kinds provided the opportunity for the inclusion of later cultural evidences.

By good fortune that happened, for in the alluvium above we see the traces of people with cultural elements not known earlier, notably the knowledge of pottery making, cremation of the dead, architecture in the form of pit houses, and, inferentially, the pursuit of agriculture. Stratigraphy clearly states these elements were later, but how much later has not been accurately determined. One can judge, as the authors have, that the age was between A.D. 500 and 1000. What we see, thus, is an evolving life style, progressing from the dependence on nature's resources to the production of at least a part of the needed food supply through plant cultivation. Of special import is the fact that in the Cienega Creek area, pottery was not known to its residents until about A.D. 1, while it was known to both the Hohokam and Mogollon peoples by the second or third century B.C.

The Cienega Valley sites shed light on another phenomenon. We tend to think of the floors of our arid valleys as stable and dating from ancient times. But now we can say that the valley bottom was three or more meters below the present surface as recently as two millennia ago, and that even after alluviation the stream creating the beds reversed its behavior several times by cutting deep channels, only to fill them up again. Happily for the archaeologist, through much of these changing topographic times, people were present, leaving traces that now challenge the scientist to merge cultural with natural history.

Although nature is a certain component in the formula of change, the uncertainty is the exact time, extent, and rapidity of that change. In the original wording of this Foreword, I noted that "the Cienega Valley sites stand as textbook examples of the blending of human and geological forces, the vertical superposition of cultural horizons in geomorphological contexts that are easily demonstrated to the learner."

But nature is restless and not content to preserve what it has built. Severe flooding in the summer of 1980 extensively modified the sites on which Eddy and Cooley worked. Old arroyo bank profiles were wiped out by the rampaging waters, and new ones created by the undercutting and carving of the channel walls. As a consequence heretofore unseen archaeological features were exposed, such as beds of cultural debris, pit houses, hearths, and burials, and the extent of culture-rich deposits was thereby widened. Furthermore, nature's removal of four meters of overburden has given the archaeologist unusually easy access to the "pay dirt" on which he thrives.

As these words are written, new investigations have been launched that will surely yield additional information to augment the findings of Eddy and Cooley.

Emil W. Haury
May 20, 1983

PREFACE

A combined program of archaeological and geological field investigation in the Empire Valley, southeastern Arizona, has resulted in the reconstruction of a sequence of cultural and environmental events that occurred over a period of approximately 3500 years to the present time. The bulk of the cultural development involved an indigenous group of people who occupied an area of two square miles near the junction of Cienega Creek and Matty Wash (sometimes called Matty Canyon).

Environmental studies were conducted by two methods: the present setting was used as an aid in understanding the interrelationships of the ecological factors operating now and as a basis for the study of past changes. Based on the reports of specialists, data on past environmental features such as the alluvial geology, shrub cover, and the mammalian and nonmarine molluscan remains are included in this study.

The primary approach to the correlation of the cultural and environmental data was based on the physical association of the alluvial geology and the archaeological components, charcoal specimens, mammal bone material, plant pollen, and nonmarine molluscan remains contained in the deposits. This relative correlation was substantiated by a variety of dating methods: radiocarbon age determination, geologic-climatic, ceramic, and historical dating.

Intermittent archaeological investigations of the Empire Valley have been conducted by the Department of Anthropology of the University of Arizona since 1926. Initial work was carried out by Byron Cummings, who excavated two human skeletons from the floor of Cienega Creek on the Empire Ranch (McGregor 1941: 115-116). These inhumations were overlain by 3.6 m of undisturbed alluvium containing shell remains. No associated artifacts were recovered with the burials.

Later, Emil W. Haury carried on the work, and he located and described many of the sites presented in this report. A comprehensive archaeological study of the Empire Valley was subsequently made by Earl H. Swanson (1951). Haury and Edward B. Danson, accompanied by University of Arizona students, conducted exploratory testing at Arizona EE:2:30 (Arizona State Museum Site Survey; Wasley 1957), a preceramic midden containing lithic material of the Cochise culture. In addition, limited work was done at Arizona EE:2:10, a ceramic horizon pit house of the Hohokam culture (Gladwin and others 1937).

This report is based on an intensive archaeological survey of the area and three weeks of excavation (Eddy 1958). Two weeks were spent at site Arizona EE:2:30. Work concentrated on Test 3, where a pit was excavated into trash underlying a large gravel bar deposited on the bottom of Matty Wash. Approximately one week was spent at sites Arizona EE:2:34, EE:2:35, and EE:2:10. Two deeply buried fire hearths (Pits 3 and 4) at site Arizona EE:2:35 were dissected in order to study their construction and to recover artifacts and charcoal samples. About 30 cm of firmly cemented fill in a pit house at Arizona EE:2:10 was removed by undercutting into the arroyo bank, and a second pit house at Arizona EE:2:34 was completely excavated.

The geological field work involved mapping the arroyo walls of Matty Wash and Cienega Creek from their point of junction to approximately one mile upstream, totaling 4424 m mapped at a scale of one inch to 50 feet (2.54 cm to 15.15 m; Cooley 1958). Within this area, seven stratigraphic sections of the Recent alluvium were described at key points. The purpose of the geological investigation was two-fold: (1) to trace and correlate the various alluvial stratigraphic units in order to understand the sedimentary environment of the area, and (2) to record where in the alluvial stratigraphy each archaeological site was located.

In addition, Paul S. Martin of the University of Arizona Geochronology Laboratories, with the assistance of James Schoenwetter, concentrated on collecting samples of recent alluvium for extractions of pollen remains. Pollen profiles were made near geologic sections MC–5 and MC–6 (Schoenwetter 1960; Martin, Schoenwetter, and Arms 1961: 50-53).

ACKNOWLEDGMENTS

The sustained archaeological and geological field projects in Cienega Valley were financed by a grant from the Comin's Fellowship Fund administered by a committee of the Department of Anthropology, University of Arizona, and by funds donated directly from this Department. Supplementary aid was given by the Arizona State Museum in the form of equipment, expendable supplies, and photographic assistance. Radiocarbon samples were analyzed in the Carbon–14 Age Determination Laboratory of the University of Arizona and by the Shell Development Company, Exploration and Production Research Division, Houston, Texas.

Robert R. Humphrey, then with the Watershed Management Department, University of Arizona, compiled the list of dominant range grasses in the Empire Valley. Terah

L. Smiley, Department of Geosciences, University of Arizona, identified the preceramic charcoal samples. Identifications of the charred wooden construction beams from the roof of the pit house at Arizona EE:2:34 were made by C. Wes Ferguson and R. A. Wright of the University of Arizona. Robert J. Drake, then of the University of Arizona Zoology Department, identified the freshwater and land molluscs collected from the alluvium. E. Lendell Cockrum and W. J. Schaldach, Jr., also of the Zoology Department, with the assistance of James J. Hester, identified and made a basic interpretation of the ecological significance of the mammal remains.

Counseling on the study problem was given by Emil W. Haury, then head of the Department of Anthropology, University of Arizona. Thoughts concerning the Cochise culture were discussed with the late E. B. Sayles, then Curator of the Arizona State Museum, and geochronology problems were examined by Terah L. Smiley.

Much of the labor was supplied by anthropology students from the University of Arizona and workers from Patagonia, Arizona. Permission to conduct field work on the Cienega ranch was granted by the owner, J. S. Greenway of Tucson, and information, advice, and hospitality were given by the ranch operators, Fred and Harry Barnett.

The authors express their thanks to all these people who have shared in the completion of this work. Special appreciation is extended to Raymond H. Thompson, Director of the Arizona State Museum, for various services aiding publication. Sue Ruiz and Carol Heathington, of the Museum, expertly typed and coded the manuscript for telecommunication. Charles Sternberg provided final drawings for most of the illustrations, including the fence diagram (Fig. 5.1). The editorial contributions of Carol A. Gifford are to be singled out, particularly. We are especially grateful to the University of Arizona Press, with its highly competent staff, for the production of this volume.

Although the field work, laboratory analyses, and report writing were largely accomplished in the late 1950s and early 1960s, many factors intervened to prevent prompt publication. We feel, however, that in general the local environmental and cultural interpretations are still valid, and no attempt has been made to update the regional interpretation of the Cochise and Hohokam archaeology. In Appendix C, Bruce Huckell, of the Arizona State Museum, has provided more recent radiocarbon dating calibrations that pertain to the Cienega Valley deposits discussed in this monograph.

Frank W. Eddy
Maurice E. Cooley

1. CIENEGA VALLEY

An interrelationship between human culture and environment through time is evident in the area near the junction of Matty Wash and Cienega Creek in the Empire Valley of southeastern Arizona (Fig. 1.1). Archaeological sites, ranging in date from about 1000 B.C. to historical occupation, show association with the Recent alluvial floodplain deposition laid down by Cienega Creek. This relationship indicates that man was living on a ground surface that had been gradually built up by almost continuous alluviation. During the last 3500 years, this process effected a vertical spread of human material remains throughout an average thickness of 9 m of alluvium. The earliest cultural manifestations were identified as temporary and semipermanent campsites occupied by hunters and gatherers of the Cochise culture during the San Pedro stage (Sayles and Antevs 1941; Sayles 1983). Later cultural deposits, dated after A.D. 1, yielded pottery of the Hohokam agriculturalists like those then living in the Tucson area.

The human occupation occurred in a grassland environment that underwent periodic shrub cover fluctuations. Modern fauna inhabited the prairies and shrub growth along slow-moving ponded streams. Several pronounced environmental fluctuations affected the local population. The dry post–A.D. 1200 arroyo cutting probably desiccated the area in a fashion similar to current conditions, thereby eradicating the local ponded marshes and diminishing an important wild plant food supply. The succeeding wet period, with indications of a heavy ground cover, may have restored the supply of marsh plant foods but it intensified the difficulty of floodplain farming. It is possible that the apparent absence of historic Indian occupation indicates that the major emphasis on hunting and gathering of plant and animal foods from early to late within the study area may have extended to the historic period, and that the sharp environmental changes were responsible for the abandonment of the area after A.D. 1500. Inferences regarding the interrelationship of man and his natural surroundings are based on these kinds of environmental stability and change.

Information concerning the changing environment was obtained by studying the sedimentary and erosional processes associated with the deposition of the Recent alluvium, by pollen analysis, and by identifying charcoal specimens, freshwater and land snails, and the remains of animal bones. The relationships of these lines of evidence aided interpretations of past climates and of the prehistoric distribution of vegetation and wildlife. The varied cultural deposits indicated both human adaptations to the fluctuations of the environment and to social changes within the community.

The locality investigated is in the narrow V-shaped junction of Matty Wash and Cienega Creek in Sections 25 and 26, Township 18 south and Range 17 east. This area is approximately 60 miles (96.6 km) southeast of Tucson and 16 miles (25.75 km) northeast of Sonoita between the Empire and Whetstone mountains. The broad region between these mountains that is occupied by the Cienega Creek drainage system is generally termed the Empire Valley, although in older reports it has been referred to as Cienega Valley (Eddy 1958). As it is used in this report, Cienega Valley refers to the floodplain of Cienega Creek and the adjacent low ridges and terraces (Fig. 1.2).

PRESENT ENVIRONMENT

An understanding of the present terrain, climate, vegetation, and wildlife is essential to an interpretation of the environments of ancient man in the Cienega Valley. The changing environment of the valley, represented physically by arroyo cutting, is an index to the study of ancient cultures and environments.

The climate of the Empire Valley supports a moderately rich natural vegetation ranging from grasslands to woodland, in contrast to the Sonoran desert that is dominated by shrubs and cacti. The grasslands have been invaded by mesquite along the lower drainages and by oak at higher elevations. Mesquite appears to be a recent introduction into this valley.

Before 1900 the streams were sluggish, flowing through dense cienegas or bogs choked with tall grass. These ponds provided permanent and temporary homes for water-dwellers such as beaver and waterfowl. The grasslands, less affected by erosion, probably supported grazing animals throughout the past century. Grasslands mixed with oak and mesquite sheltered deer and javelina. In spite of the relatively rich supply of natural plant and animal foods available in the past, malarial conditions associated with the swampy areas may have been an obstacle to permanent human settlement.

Physiography

The Empire and Whetstone mountains reach altitudes of over 2121 m and consist of igneous, metamorphic, and sedimentary rocks varying in age from Precambrian to Mesozoic. Between the mountain fronts and the floodplain

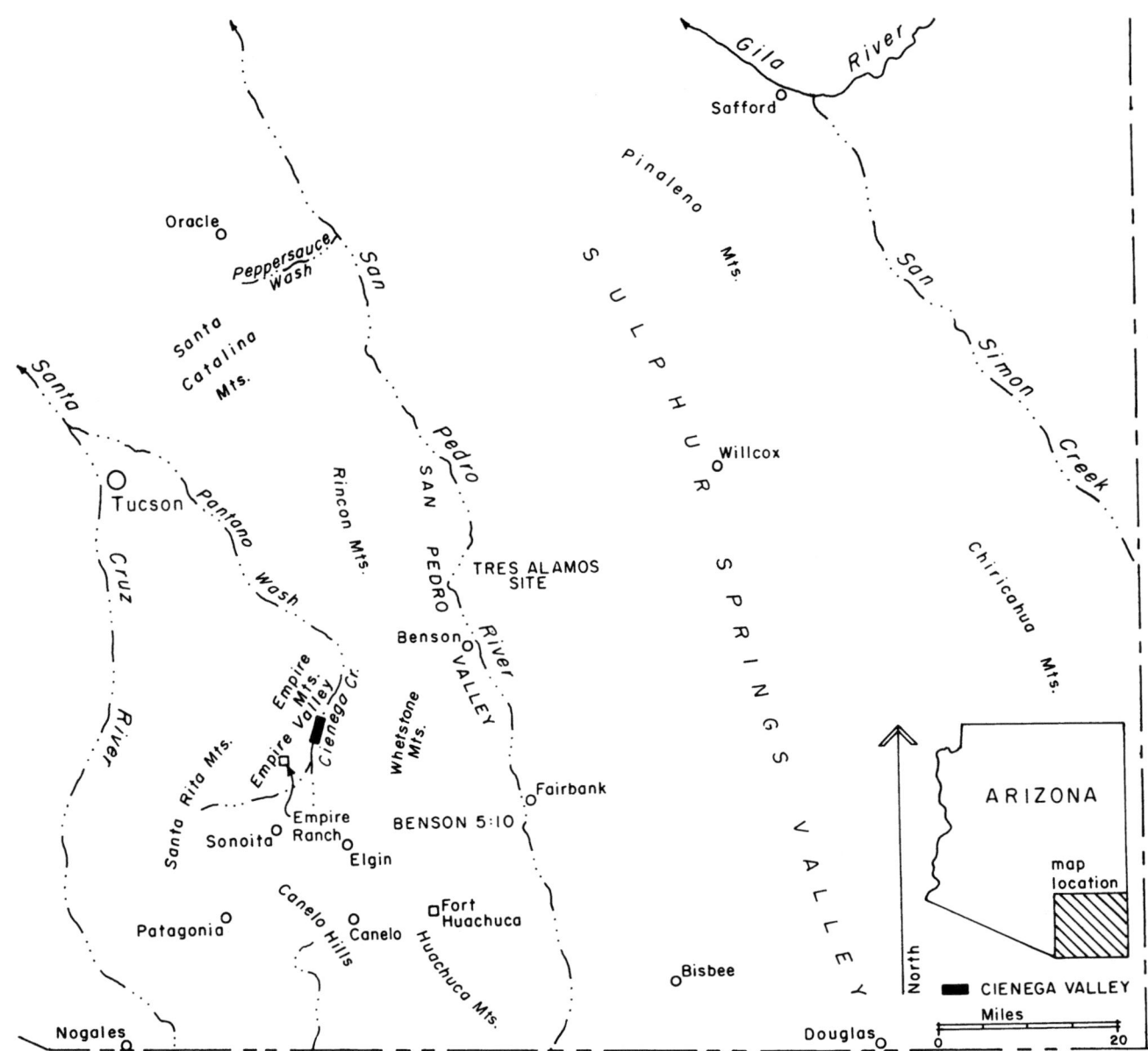

Figure 1.1. Cienega Creek Basin, southeastern Arizona. The study area is shown in Figure 1.3.

of Cienega Creek are a series of terraces that have been formed on Cretaceous rocks and late Tertiary and Pleistocene valley fill. The terraces have a slope of approximately 150 feet (45.5 m) per mile. Below the lowest terrace, the Recent floodplain of Cienega Valley has been built up by the master Cienega Creek and its tributaries, including Matty Wash and other ephemeral streams (Fig. 1.3).

In the area studied the altitude of Cienega Valley is approximately 1273 m. In the 1950s, Cienega Creek, except the stretch near site Arizona EE:2:36, was perennial, with a flow of more than 1.893 kl per minute. A small amount of water issued from a seep near Section MC–5 and flowed 151.5 m down Matty Wash.

The present valley of Cienega Creek is the result of several stages of development. Initial valley formation occurred after uplift and large scale faulting during the middle and late Tertiary. These structural movements outlined many of the present land forms in southern Arizona. The valley was filled with hundreds of feet of gravel deposits. Erosion, principally during the Pleistocene and probably the result of regional uplift, carved several prominent terraces and removed many of the deposits, exposing Cretaceous rocks along the creek channel. The floodplain of Cienega Creek was built to its present level in late Recent time by the deposition of several alluvial units.

Climate

The present climate of southeastern Arizona is part of a larger unit of a tropical and subtropical desert area defined by Trewartha (1956: 39) as a dry climate. Although there are no weather records for Cienega Valley, precipitation and temperature are estimated from records of stations maintained in nearby areas (Table 1.1). Cienega Valley

Figure 1.2. Cienega Valley: area of confluence of Matty Wash and Cienega Creek. The Empire Mountains form the skyline.

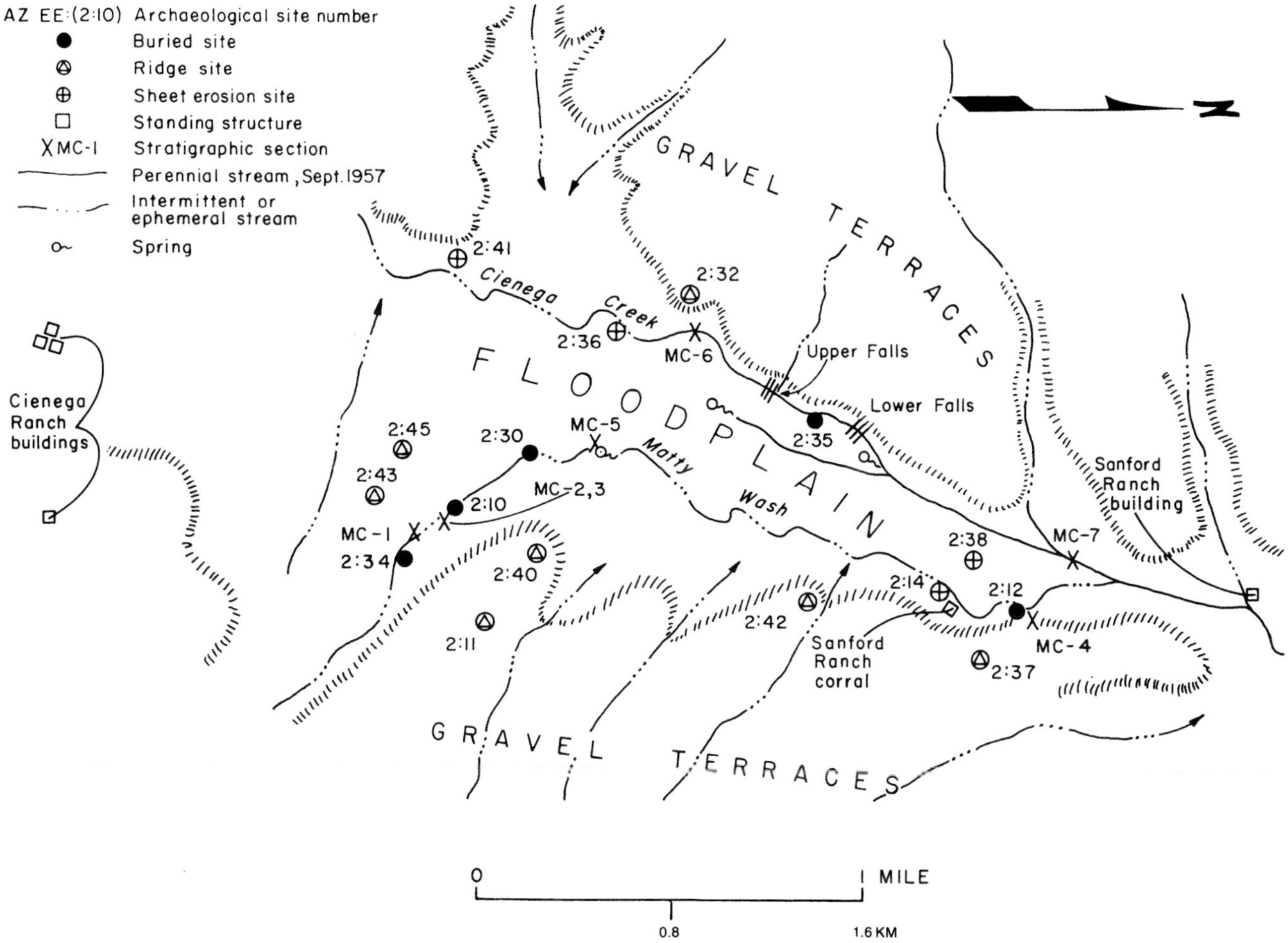

Figure 1.3. Cienega Valley: drainage patterns, physiographic features, archaeological sites, and stratigraphic sections.

TABLE 1.1
Climatic Data from Stations Near the Empire Valley

Data	Stations					
	Benson	Canelo	Elgin	Fairbank	Ft. Huachuca	Cienega Valley[a]
Altitude (m)	1091	1515	1485	1170	1413	1273
Years of record	1903–1959	1910–1959	1912–1959	1909–1959	1900–1959	
Mean annual temperature (°C)	17.1	13.3[b]			16.5[b]	16.0 (approx.)
Mean annual precipitation (cm)	28.12	46.97	37.90	28.98	41.78[b]	31–36
Mean annual snowfall (cm)[c]	4.1	27.2	14.7	5.3		5.0
Average number of days with more than 0.03 cm of precipitation[c]	40	63	47	43		45
Average length of growing season (days)[c]	226	170	164	170		170
Last killing spring frost[c]	May 11	June 4	June 5	May 23		June 1
First killing fall frost[c]	Oct. 8	Sept. 24	Oct. 1	Oct. 2		Oct. 1

a. Estimated from records of other stations in table.
b. Incomplete records.
c. Smith (1956).

probably receives between 30.5 cm and 35.6 cm of annual precipitation. The valley has a mean annual temperature of 15.6°C (60°F), with a growing season of 170 or more days. Snowfall is light and negligible as a factor of soil moisture. The low annual precipitation restricts the growing of corn and other crops without irrigation.

The precipitation pattern for southeastern Arizona has two semiannual peaks separated by intermittent periods of dryness. Most of the rain occurs from December through February and in July and August. Summer rains are brought by a shift to the northwest of the subtropical anticyclone in the Gulf-Caribbean area (Bryson 1957: 6). This pattern is replaced in winter by a westerly jet stream shifting southward to a mean position of 35° north latitude. Winter precipitation is caused by migratory low pressure systems and troughs of low pressure associated with this jet wind (Bryson 1957: 4). Dry periods between the winter and summer rainfalls result from the lag of one pattern behind the other.

Summer storms are formed as the result of a buildup of thunderhead cloud masses that peak in a short time and distribute precipitation in relatively large local areas. The sudden, intense nature of these storms produces rapid runoff and gully erosion that is aided by the inadequate protection of the vegetation cover.

Winter storms are marked by the appearance of large, dark cloud fronts. Winter precipitation is more general, lasts longer, and is less intense than the summer rains. Increased cloudiness diminishes the high annual evaporation rate, which ranges between 1.8 m and 2.1 m (Smith 1956: 93), resulting in a greater amount of moisture remaining in the soil for plant use.

Vegetation

Paul S. Martin

The Empire Valley is bordered by the Sonoran desert on the west and the Chihuahuan desert on the east. The valley is dominated by grassland and is located above the lower Sonoran life zone and below oak woodland (Fig. 1.4). Below 909 m is the warm Sonoran desert, characterized chiefly by shrubs such as creosote bush (*Larrea*), acacia (*Acacia greggii* and *A. constricta*), brittle bush (*Encelia*), and ocotillo (*Fouquieria splendens*), and some trees and cacti such as palo verde (*Cercidium floridum* and *C. microphyllum*) and saguaro (*Cereus giganteus*).

Outliers of the relatively cool Chihuahuan desert are found on limestone hills and alluvial slopes of limestone-derived soils in the San Pedro Valley and parts of the Empire Valley. These outliers of the Chihuahuan desert are also shrub-dominated, but do not have the abundance of species found in the Sonoran desert. Creosote bush, tar bush (*Flourensia cernua*), mortonia (*Mortonia scabrella*), and ocotillo are among the dominant species.

The types of vegetation found in the Empire Valley include mesquite woods or bosque on the alluvial floodplains, grassland on the broad slopes between the floodplains and the mountains, and forest above 2273 m on the north slopes of the Santa Rita Mountains.

Fred Barnett (Eddy 1958: 20) reported that within the last 50 years the floodplain along Cienega Creek has been invaded by dense stands of mesquite (*Prosopis juliflora*). Only occasional dense head-high patches of sacaton (*Sporobolus*) remain, because this large bunchgrass, lacking

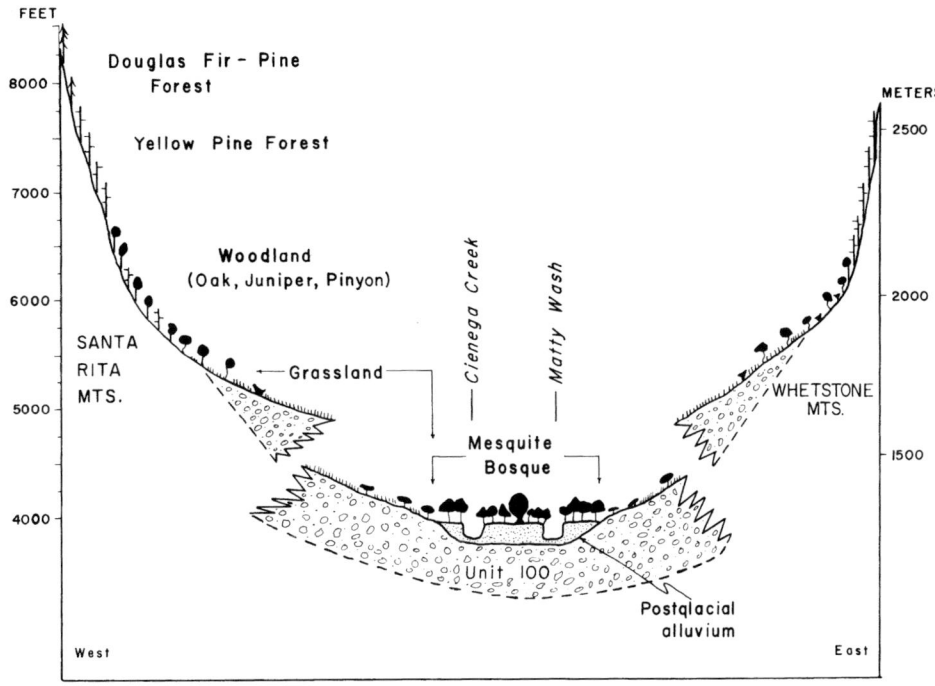

Figure 1.4. Diagrammatic profile of Empire Valley vegetation.

the typical mesquite taproot system, is unable to reach water in areas where the water table has been lowered by deep arroyo cutting.

The mesquite trees attain maximum size in the Empire Valley at the confluence of Cienega Creek and Matty Wash. The trees are more than 8 m high, form a continuous crown cover, and are spaced 1.5 m to 3 m apart. The dense shade eliminates most understory herbs. Other trees such as cottonwood (*Populus fremontii*), willow (*Salix*), ash (*Fraxinus*), black walnut (*Juglans*), and shrubby batamote (*Baccharis glutinosa*) grow chiefly in wet areas along the streams.

The gramas and other grasses (Table 1.2) inhabiting the broad slopes of the Empire Valley resemble those of the desert grasslands (Marshall 1957) that are distributed throughout parts of southeastern Arizona, southwestern New Mexico, and the east flank of the Sierra Madre Occidental in northern Mexico (Shreve 1939: 8). In many places, especially on north-facing slopes, the grass cover is interrupted by patches of desert shrubs. Various shrubs, especially shrub-size mesquite, are dominant locally. *Juniperus monosperma* occupies the north slopes of hillsides near the Matty Wash-Cienega Creek junction. On Cretaceous rocks where soil is thin, grasses may be replaced by acacias, mesquite, Mormon tea (*Ephedra trifurca*), yucca (*Yucca elata*), octillo, and agave. Above elevations of 1394 m, mesquite declines; mimosa, bear grass (*Nolina*), and alligator juniper (*Juniperus deppeana*) are infrequent; the gramas are luxurient; and the appearance of oak (*Quercus emoryi* and *Q. oblongifolia*) along stream channels and north-facing slopes of ridges marks the lower boundary of the forest zone.

Above 1636 m grow various oaks, alligator juniper, manzanita (*Arctostaphlos*), and pinyon (*Pinus cembroides*).

TABLE 1.2
Dominant Range Grasses in the Empire Valley*

Species	Common name
Aristida divaricata Humb. and Bonpl.	Poverty three-awn
Andropogon	Texas bear grass
Andropogon barbinodis Lag.	Cane bear grass
Bouteloua chondrosioides (H.B.K.) Benth.	Sprucetop grama
Bouteloua curtipendula (Michx.) Torr.	Side oats grama
Bouteloua filiformis (Fourn.) Griffiths.	Slender grama
Bouteloua gracilis (H.B.K.) Lag.	Blue grama
Bouteloua hirsuta Lag.	Hairy grama
Hilaria belangeri (Steud.) Nash.	Curly mesquite
Eragrostis intermedia Hitchc.	Plains love grass

*Compiled by Robert R. Humphrey, Watershed Management Department, University of Arizona (1958).

Pine is not found below 1636 m. Tree height and density increase with elevation, and above 1970 m forests dominated by Arizona pine appear on the north-facing slopes of the Santa Rita Mountains. Above 2273 m Douglas fir (*Pseudotsuga*), white pine (*Pinus reflexa*), and ultimately, white fir (*Abies concolor*) and aspen (*Populus tremuloides*), may occur. This montane forest is limited to the peak region of the Santa Rita Mountains. Viewed from the air, only the highest north-facing slopes of the Whetstone Mountains seem to be covered with forests; the south-facing slopes are covered wtih woodland and chaparral.

Wildlife

The wildlife of Cienega Valley is similar to that throughout southeastern Arizona. Jackrabbit (*Lepus*) and desert cottontail (*Sylvilagus*) are present in the mesquite woods along the main drainage courses, as well as on the grass-covered ridges, which are also a habitat of kangaroo rats (*Dipodomys*). Javelina (*Pecari*) and mule deer (*Odocoileus hemionus*) browse in the mixed oak and grass near the Whetstone Mountains, and occasionally on the floodplain of Cienega Creek. The more open grasslands at the base of the Mustang Mountains support small herds of antelope (*Antilocapra americana*). Skunk (*Mephitis*) and porcupine (*Erethizon*) tunnel in the arroyo walls. Badgers (*Taxidea*), which prey on domestic fowl, inhabit the alluvial floodplains. Larger predators such as coyote (*Canis latrans*) and mountain lion (*Felis concolor*) prowl throughout the area. It is important to note that although Di Peso (1951: 12) reported the prehistoric occurrence of bison (*Bison bison*) at the Babocomari village site near the Huachuca Mountains, they have not been reported in the Empire Valley within the historical past and no bison remains were found in the late Recent deposits.

Environmental Conditions of the Historic Past

Travelers and residents of the Empire Valley were valuable sources of information concerning environmental features they observed during their lifetimes. Many of their descriptions of conditions provided an opportunity to record seasonal and long-term changes that were not available from other sources nor apparent during the short field investigation.

During the mid-nineteenth century, John Bartlett (1854) made a boundary survey between the United States and Mexico. In September of 1851, he passed through an area that is believed to have been the Empire Valley. Bartlett (1854: 383) described the area as a plateau countryside that supported a short grass cover similar to that of the western prairies. The drainages contained swamps and pools of water surrounded by luxuriant stands of head-high grass and groves of small oaks. The survey party encountered wildlife such as mustangs, deer, antelope, and stream trout.

Information from Orion Enzenberg, a local rancher, provided additional environmental evidence for the late nineteenth and early twentieth centuries. According to Enzenberg, during this period the valley of Cienega Creek was not trenched, but consisted of a grass-covered floodplain containing swamps or cienegas, a few of which remained unentrenched in the 1950s (Martin, Schoenwetter, and Arms 1961, pl. 2). These boggy meadows forced the construction of a mining road to skirt the floodplain and follow the high ground along the flanks of adjacent ridges. The cienegas held beaver and, in season, were resting points for migratory waterfowl. Enzenberg also had heard that the valley was never permanently occupied by Indians because of malarial conditions. "In the old days, the settlers used to take a lot of quinine," he said.

At the end of the nineteenth century, slight environmental changes in the Empire Valley caused arroyo cutting, which in turn drained the cienegas. This period of erosion presumably started earlier in the surrounding regions (Bryan 1925; Antevs 1955). Arroyo cutting may have developed more slowly in the Empire Valley because the ample ground cover helped to check erosion. A late age for the arroyo cutting is supported by evidence from local rancher E. Hilton, who related that when he was a boy, "it was possible to drive across the valley floor in a buggy without obstructions." If Hilton's estimated age of 65 (in 1958) is correct, arroyo cutting may not have started until after the 1890s. Fred Barnett recalled that in 1905 "the Matty Wash was not a third as deep as it is today." It seems likely that cutting in the Empire Valley began between 1890 and 1905, with 1900 as the approximate date for the beginning of arroyo trenching along Cienega Creek. During the last 50 years, Fred Barnett has also observed a general replacement of grasslands by mesquite woods along the drainages and a drying up of the cienegas that formerly existed along Cienega Creek. The arroyo cutting has resulted in the general lowering of the water table and the end of floodplain farming without irrigation.

GEOLOGICAL STRATIGRAPHY

The Cretaceous rocks bordering the floodplain of Cienega Creek are present throughout the area, either on the surface or at a depth covered only by valley fill materials. They are the only rocks that have been subjected to low-grade metamorphism. An old valley fill (Unit 100), probably of Pleistocene age, overlies the Cretaceous rocks and is exposed in several places in the arroyo walls beneath the late Recent alluvium (see Fig. 2.16). The youngest sediments comprising the late Recent alluvium (Units 1–7) are floodplain deposits that form a thin mantle on the older rocks (Fig. 1.5).

Cretaceous Rocks

The rocks of Cretaceous age that constitute the bedrock underlying Cienega Creek consist of a sequence more than 50 m thick of alternating cross-bedded arkosic and flat-bedded silty sandstones. Some of the individual units of these lenticular, thick-bedded to very thick-bedded deposits can be traced across the area investigated. A buff, limy sandstone bed containing abundant fossils of the genus *Oystrea* crops out approximately 0.25 mile (0.4 km) west of Cienega Creek. The Cretaceous rocks represent nearshore and floodplain types of depositional environments.

Pleistocene Deposits

The Pleistocene deposits (Unit 100) are chiefly stream-laid sand and gravel that form the terraces enclosing Cienega Valley. Unit 100 was exposed in only a few places along the flanks of the valley in 1957, because the arroyos were not of sufficient depth in the center of the valley to expose them.

Unit 100 ranges in color from pale red to moderate yellowish-brown, is poorly sorted, and weakly to firmly cemented by calcareous materials (see Figs. 2.9g, 5.1). Limestone nodules and well-developed caliche zones are commonly observed in the unit. The gravel has a maximum size of approximately 31 cm, but most pieces are less than 10 cm across the long dimension. The matrix is composed mainly of quartz sand that is rounded to subangular in

Figure 1.5. West bank of Cienega Creek at Section MC–6.

shape, and less angular than the sand grains in the overlying Recent deposits. A few thin silty layers composed of mudchips occur throughout. Unit 100 is cross-bedded with lenticular layers less than 1.2 m thick.

A few soil zones or residual mantles derived from local sources have been preserved at the top of Unit 100 and beneath the late Recent deposits. These residual-soil materials vary from 15.2 cm to 91.4 cm thick, and have formed indiscriminately across the sand and gravel beds. The zone is generally structureless and contains some carbonaceous material and limestone nodules. The soil zone was probably formed during the late Pleistocene and early Recent.

Late Recent Alluvium

The late Recent floodplain alluvium in Cienega Valley mainly consists of a gradational and intertonguing sequence of deposits; Units 3 and 5 were laid down by streams and Units 4 and 6 accumulated in swamps and ponds (see Appendixes A and B). These deposits show variations in lithology both in cross-sectional and longitudinal profiles (Fig. 1.6). Units 5 and 6, and the lower part of Unit 4, are closely related depositionally and form the basal part of the alluvial sequence. Unit 3 and the upper part of Unit 4, similarly related, make up the bulk of the late Recent deposits that are exposed in Cienega Valley. Unit 3 is overlain by Unit 2, which is represented in most places by a soil zone. Unit 1, overlying Unit 2 and older alluvial deposits, was laid down before the cutting of the present arroyos. Unit 7 is not a stratigraphic unit like the others; rather it represents an accumulation of a residual-colluvial mantle along the sides of the valley. Of all the alluvial units, only Unit 2 can be recognized in the nearby drainages to Cienega Creek; it has been named the Sanford formation, after the old Sanford Ranch of Cienega Valley.

Unit 7

Unit 7 is the oldest Recent sedimentary unit deposited in this part of the valley. It usually overlies Unit 100, but in places it has been preserved in depressions developed in the Cretaceous bedrock. This unit, a residual deposit, is composed of material derived principally from adjacent older rocks. The unit is structureless, mainly consisting of sand or sandy silt containing angular pebble-sized fragments, and it is weakly bonded by a calcareous cement. Limestone nodules are common. Unit 7 is generally pale brown, but near site Arizona EE:2:10 it is grayish orange-pink. Some carbonaceous material, trash, and scrapers were found in Unit 7 near Arizona EE:2:12.

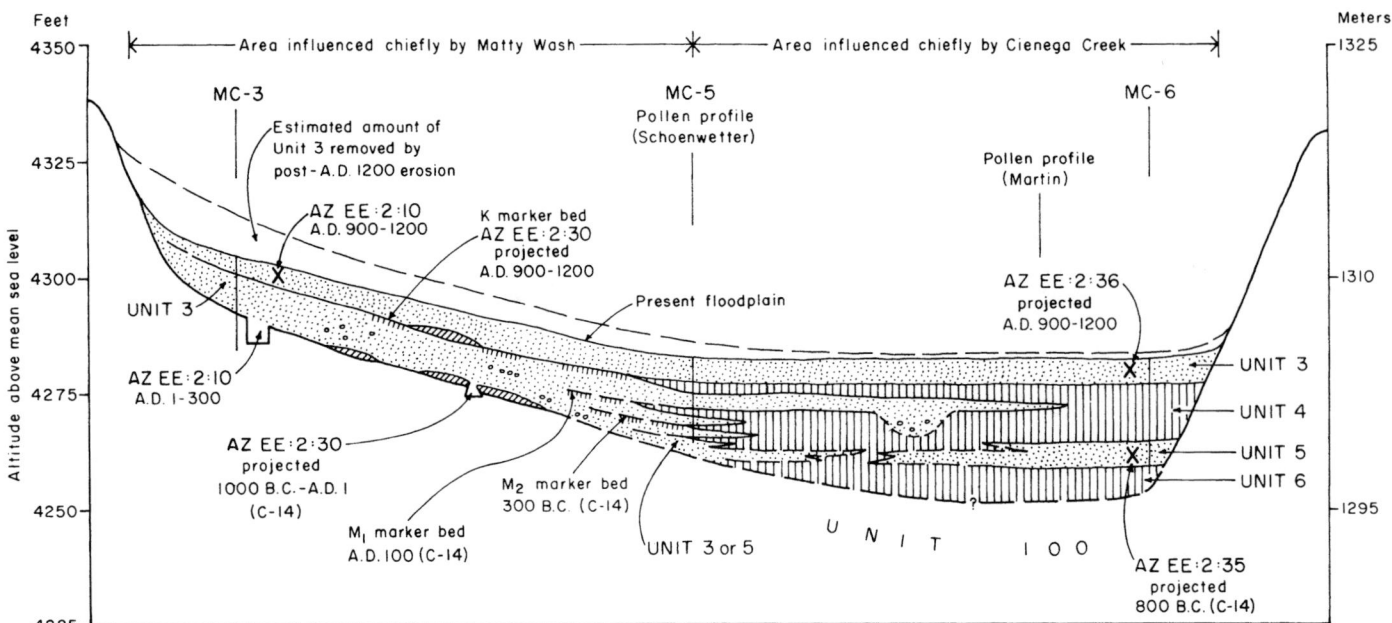

Figure 1.6. Schematic cross section of Cienega Valley, illustrating the intertonguing relationships between sediments and archaeological sites.

Unit 6

This grayish unit probably underlies most of the area, although it is exposed only along the sides of the valley (Fig. 1.6). The deposit is chiefly a mud, but its composition ranges from an impure clay to a silt containing some fine-grained sand. The unit is thinly bedded, but in places it is contorted, suggesting primary slumpage. Compaction after deposition has given the bedding a slight dip toward the center of the valley. Unit 6 is plastic when wet and weakly cemented. Molluscs and plant remains were found scattered throughout the unit. The intertonguing between Unit 6 and Unit 5 is shown in most of the exposures along Cienega Creek.

Unit 5

Fluvial deposits of Unit 5 overlie Unit 6, with the common contact partly gradational and partly intertonguing (see Fig. 2.5). In a few places along Cienega Creek, however, small channels filled with sand and gravel were eroded into the top of Unit 6 (see Fig. 2.6). The sandy sediments grade and intertongue laterally and upward with the muddy sediments of Unit 4. In places along Matty Wash where Unit 4 is absent, Unit 5 is overlain by Unit 3. At Section MC-5, deposits below the M_2 marker bed can be correlated with either Unit 5 or Unit 3 because of lithologic similarity to both units. Elsewhere, Unit 5 is overlain by Unit 4.

Although the general composition of Unit 5 is a sand or silty sand, pale yellowish-brown, it varies from a sandy mud to a sandy gravel. The sand is fine-grained and weakly bonded by a calcareous cement. The unit is characterized by small-scale cross bedding, but large-scale cross bedding may be seen at Section MC-7. Silt and a few mud beds similar to Unit 6 occur in the lower part of the unit.

In 1957, Unit 5, between the upper and lower falls on Cienega Creek at Arizona EE:2:35, contained artifacts and many fire pits dating to the San Pedro stage (see Fig. 2.5). Elsewhere along the creek only charcoal fragments and some scanty trash(?) lenses were preserved. Along Matty Wash, however, no evidences of human occupation in Unit 5 were observed.

Unit 4

The muddy deposits of Unit 4, often called "cienega beds," were laid down in the shallow lakes and swampy areas that occupied large parts of Cienega Valley. The unit consists mostly of thin-bedded brownish-gray mud with stringers of silty sand and carbonaceous material. The muddy beds are concentrated in the western part of the valley, thinning toward the east by intertonguing with sandy Unit 3. The almost pure peat layers at Section MC-5 along Matty Wash may be tongues of Unit 4 that are interbedded with Unit 3 deposits.

Individual beds in Unit 4 extend laterally for more than 50 m, in contrast to the lenticular beds of Units 3 and 5 that extend laterally for only short distances. Several beds of Unit 4 were traced for as long as 0.25 mile (0.4 km) near the lower falls of Cienega Creek. The X marker bed, which forms the upper contact of Unit 4 in the northern area (see Fig. 2.5), is a well-displayed horizon in the arroyo walls.

Only one San Pedro stage occupation site, Arizona EE:2:12, was found in Unit 4. The site was in a sandy layer that was traced approximately 46 m to the south, where it tongued out into the typical mud of the unit.

Unit 3

Unit 3 is the most complex of the alluvial units because it consists of several subunits of fluvial-laid sediments separated by soil profiles. The unit is characterized by channeling that is more common and better developed along Matty Wash, where sharply defined and steep-sided channels were cut into the underlying deposits of Unit 4 along Cienega Creek and into Unit 100 near Section MC–1.

Unit 3 is composed of three types of deposits: (1) cross-bedded sand and gravel that make up the channel deposits; (2) structureless sandy silt similar to loess; and (3) dark gray silt beds, probably old soils. Two prominent soil zones traceable laterally over much of Cienega Valley were used for correlation: the X marker bed in the northeastern part and the K marker bed in the southern part of the area. Many of the soil zones of Unit 3 may be traced into the cienega deposits of Unit 4 (Fig. 1.6).

Unit 3 varies from pale red to pale brown. It is weakly bonded by a calcareous cement and is more consolidated in the southeastern part of the area. By intertonguing with Unit 4, the unit thins to the west and is composed of finer sediments near Cienega Creek.

Evidence of Hohokam occupation was indicated in all parts of Unit 3. These sites were located in the silty beds, and they were not found (or were not preserved) near channels or on soil zones. The silty beds may represent drier and more favorable habitation conditions than the damp soils or stream channels. No remains of the earlier San Pedro stage were found.

Unit 2, Sanford Formation

The deposition of the alluvial Sanford formation took place after an erosional interval that removed large portions of Unit 3. The formation is primarily a soil zone developed on the floodplain of Cienega Valley. However, fluvial deposits along the flanks of the valley and the filling of two deep channels with Unit 2 deposits indicate some deposition, in addition to soil development. The channels filled by Unit 2 deposits represent an older period of arroyo cutting.

The brownish-gray soil zone is mainly silt or sandy silt reaching thicknesses of 1 m. The unit contains some poorly formed limy nodules and is weakly bonded by a calcareous cement. Many freshwater snails and small molluscs were collected from the soil zone.

The bottom part of the channel fill at Arizona EE:2:10 contained about 2 m of gravel sediments, but the gravel was not present in the channels exposed near the confluence of Matty Wash and Cienega Creek. The main body of the fill of all the channels was thin-bedded silt and sandy silt containing mudchips and evidence of alternating flooding, deposition, and drying. A few layers of carbonaceous material approximately 0.3 cm thick are scattered throughout the silty beds. Some differential compaction is indicated by the beds that dip gently toward the center of the channels.

Unit 1

The youngest alluvium of the area, except for the modern stream-laid sand and gravel, was deposited during the initial stage of the present period of arroyo cutting. The unit is preserved as a thin mantle ranging from 0.15 m to 1.22 m in thickness. Locally, small channels cutting into the underlying units have a depth of 1.83 m. Unit 1 is thicker and contains more gravel near Matty Wash than in the area near Cienega Creek. The unit is mainly composed of silty sand and sand containing pebbles scattered throughout the unit, concentrated as lenses or found along the channel bottoms. Some wind-deposited sand, the only eolian deposit of the area, was laid down near Arizona EE:2:10 (Figs. 1.6, 2.7).

2. CULTURAL SEQUENCE

Many San Pedro preceramic and Hohokam ceramic sites have been buried by the late Recent floodplain deposits of Cienega Valley. The few historic sites on the floodplain are associated with the alluviation (Units 1 and 2) that took place prior to the formation of the present arroyos. Evidence of human occupation on the floodplain is shown in profile by exposures in the arroyo walls and as concentrations of cultural debris in areas stripped by sheet erosion. In addition, prehistoric sites occur on the terraces bordering the floodplain (see Figs. 1.3, 2.16).

ARCHAEOLOGICAL SITES
Preceramic Sites

In 1957, three San Pedro stage sites, Arizona EE:2:12, 2:30, and 2:35, were overlain by an average of 5 m of alluvium. These buried stations were characterized by a distinctive assemblage of stone and bone tools, deep and shallow rock-filled cooking pits, and trash middens.

Arizona EE:2:12

A buried station, composed of a series of campsite components, was exposed at two places in the lower half of the alluvial sequence in the east bank of Matty Wash, 0.25 mile (0.4 km) above its junction with Cienega Creek. The older remains were collected from residual-soil material (Unit 7), which underlay Unit 5 at this location. The upper 30.5 cm of the residual soil material contained trash(?) from which a single sidescraper (Fig. 2.1a) was recovered. In a silty sand bed located stratigraphically near the middle of Unit 4, younger material, consisting of a sidescraper and stemmed point (Fig. 2.1b, c), was associated with an unexcavated hearth lens. Among the contents of an excavated hearth area were numerous basalt and other fire-cracked rocks, an assortment of grinding tools (Fig. 2.1d), chalcedony workshop chips, and an unworked deer antler tine. Some scattered hearth material and artifacts (Fig. 2.1e, f) were found in the lower part of Unit 3.

Arizona EE:2:30

An extensive midden was located at the base of the west bank in Matty Wash about 1.23 miles (2.0 km) above the junction with Cienega Creek (Fig. 2.2). The midden was 61 cm thick and extended more than 36 m laterally. Pits occurring within the trash midden were dug more than 61 cm into the underlying compact Unit 100 (Figs. 2.3, 2.4).

The trash and pits overlain by Unit 3 were in a depression that was part of an erosion surface cut on Unit 100. A zone of weathering was observed on the upper surface of the trash, suggesting subaerial exposure after final abandonment of the site. The general lack of high organic content in the overlying deposits indicated that there was little mixing between the trash and the overlying Unit 3 material, although older deposits of Unit 3 (or Unit 5) were being laid down concurrently a short distance to the west and northwest (downstream) near Section MC–5.

Arizona EE:2:35

Cultural material consisting of fire hearths and a trash zone was exposed in the east bank of Cienega Creek near the lower falls (Fig. 2.5). Two shallow basin hearths were found within Unit 7 immediately below the falls. Between 15 m and 61 m upstream from this point, three other fire pits (numbered 3, 4, 5) were preserved in the sandy deposits of Unit 5. These pits were associated with a trash zone, near the top of Unit 5, that contained charcoal and bone identified as mule deer, antelope, and jackrabbit.

Two deep cooking pits were excavated in order to study their method of construction and recover their contents. Cooking Pit 3 contained quantities of heat-fractured stones and disintegrated charcoal, which was collected for radiocarbon anaysis (Table 3.1, sample Sh–5356). Cooking Pit 4 (Fig. 2.6) was similar in construction but also contained two shallow-basin milling stones and identifiable charcoal fragments (Table 2.1, sample A–89; Table 3.1, samples A–87 and A–89). Pit 5, a shallow-basin hearth located at the contact between Unit 5 and the overlying Unit 4, produced no artifactual material or carbon samples.

Later visits to Arizona EE:2:35 disclosed that lateral erosion had destroyed Pits 3, 4, and 5. Because Cienega Creek is continually cutting into its east bank, however, at least five other shallow hearths associated with the trash zone have been exposed.

Ceramic Sites

Sites containing pottery, dating after A.D. 1, consisted of buried pit houses, buried trash zones, sheet erosion sites, sites on ridges, and buried historic remains. They have been placed in stratigraphic sequence and dated by their distinctive pottery types (see Table 2.4).

Buried Pit Houses

Two examples of pit house architecture were exposed in cross section 152 m apart in the east bank of Matty Wash. The older structure of the Vahki–Estrella phase at Arizona EE:2:10 was originally dug into Unit 100 prior to the deposition of Unit 3b in this locality (Fig. 2.7). The younger pit

Figure 2.1. Stone tools from preceramic surveyed sites: *a*, thick flake sidescraper, Unit 7; *b*, thick flake sidescraper, Unit 4c; *c*, stemmed point, Unit 4c; *d*, handstone, Lens 2, Unit 4b; *e*, small slab grinding stone, Unit 3c; *f*, handstone, Unit 3c; *g*, shallow-basin milling stone, Pit 4, Unit 5. All tools are from Arizona EE:2:12 except *g*, which is from Arizona EE:2:35. Length of *c* is 7.7 cm.

house of the Cañada del Oro-Rillito phase at Arizona EE:2:34 was excavated from a local erosion surface ("S") developed in the middle of Unit 3 (Fig. 2.8). Sections of the adobe wall of the pit house curved over onto this erosion surface, indicating the stratigraphic position of the structure.

Buried Trash Zones

Two deposits of cultural debris at Arizona EE:2:10 occurred within Unit 3 stratigraphically above the pit house component (Fig. 2.7). The lower zone (Unit 3b), assigned to the late Pioneer period, consisted of a thin admixture of charcoal, cremated human bone fragments, and tools. Two

Figure 2.2. Matty Wash at Arizona EE:2:30. The San Pedro stage midden is exposed at the base of the bank to the left of the excavation.

in situ cremations and a cache of tools were associated with this zone, perhaps representing a continuation of the underlying pit house occupation as the Unit 3 alluvium was being laid down. This cultural deposit probably equated with other, less distinctive trash lenses both in the lower part of Unit 3 and at the contact between this unit and Unit 100. In the east bank of Matty Wash these trash lenses extended downstream 91 m toward Arizona EE:2:30.

The upper trash zone (Unit 3a), containing Rincon phase material, was near the top of Unit 3 and was associated with the K marker bed. Scattered tools, red-on-brown sherds, and several in situ cremations and burials were found in this trash zone. No direct evidence of burial pits was noticed during the field work. One cremation was of crucial importance in assigning a phase designation to the upper part of Unit 3. In 1958, Emil Haury found two bowls, identified as Rincon Red-on-brown (Fig. 2.15a, c), associated with and inverted directly over a pocket of burned human bone. Although the cremation pit could have been dug down from a higher surface (the top of Unit 3), this does not appear to have happened.

A ceramic component at Arizona EE:2:30 was at the same stratigraphic horizon as the upper trash zone at Arizona EE:2:10. Here a single pit containing an upright flexed skeleton was associated with a gravel lens and a soil zone (the K marker bed). Scattered within these beds were charcoal, tools, and red-on-brown sherds that equated typologically with the pottery from the cremation in the upper zone at Arizona EE:2:10.

Sheet Erosion Sites

A number of ceramic-producing sites located adjacent to the arroyos were exposed by lateral stripping of Units 1, 2, and the uppermost part of Unit 3. These sites revealed occupation of the floodplain during the deposition of Unit 2 and the upper part of Unit 3, and possibly during the time of erosion that occurred between Units 3 and 2.

It was unfortunate for our purposes that only two of these sites yielded painted ceramic sherds that indicated phase and time placement. Arizona EE:2:36, which was occupied during the Rincon phase, was probably representative of most of the sites in this physical environment. Arizona EE:2:14 presented a more complex situation; in this area, accelerated sheet erosion exposed more deeply buried ceramic trash extending back to the Cañada del Oro phase. It is important to note, however, that this erosion did not cut below the X marker bed.

Although no sherds were observed in situ, the Tanque Verde phase occupation at Arizona EE:2:14 was most likely associated with the Sanford formation (Unit 2) or the top of Unit 3. Evidence for this interpretation was obtained from chance finds of sherds at nonsite locations within the

Figure 2.3. West bank of Matty Wash at Test 1, Arizona EE:2:30. The San Pedro stage midden is exposed at the base of the bank. A dog burial was located on top of the pedestal of midden material.

Figure 2.4. Test 3, Arizona EE:2:30. Dark midden underlies the modern stream gravel and overlies Unit 100.

Figure 2.5. East bank of Cienega Creek above the lower falls at Arizona EE:2:35. The alluvial units are especially thin-bedded, and the shallow channel is filled with Unit 2 deposits.

Figure 2.6. Cooking Pit 4 after excavation at Arizona EE:2:35.

TABLE 2.1
Identification of Charcoal and Beams from Archaeological Sites in Cienega Valley

Provenience	Identification	Comments
Arizona EE:2:30[a]		
Test 2, Midden	*Quercus* sp.	Oak
Test 3, Pit 11 (A–85)	*Prosopis* sp.	Mesquite
	Quercus sp.	Oak
Pit 13	*Prosopis* sp.	Mesquite
Pit 14 (A–86a–c)	*Prosopis* sp.	Mesquite
Arizona EE:2:35[a]		
Pit 4 (A–89a–c)	*Prosopis* sp.	Mesquite
	Undetermined	Specimen unidentified
	Undetermined	Specimen unidentified
Arizona EE:2:34[b]		
Sample 1, Roof beam	*Fraxinus*	Three fragments of one piece of ash wood; radius approximately 2.5 cm; contains more than 50 rings indicating complacent growth.
Sample 2, Beam	*Salix* or *Populus*	All fragments are from one stem showing five or six rings; ring width is between 0.2 cm and 0.3 cm; complacent growth indicated.
Thatch	Grass or grasslike plants	
Sample 3, Beams	Conifer	Possibly *Pinus ponderosa*
	Salix or *Populus*	Similar in appearance to Sample 2, beam.
Sample 4, Beam	*Fraxinus*	One log, 3 to 4 cm in diameter, showing more than 50 rings.
Sample 5, Roof beam (or wood) from ramp)	*Fraxinus* 1	One log, fragmented; pieces with 1 to 3 cm radius; showing six or seven large rings; complacent growth indicated.
	Fraxinus 2	Fragments with 1 to 2 cm radius, showing 10 to 20 rings; rings indicate slower growth than those of *Fraxinus* 1.
	Juniperus	Possibly 50 to 100 rings present; sensitive growth indicated.
	Salix or *Populus*	Three or more small fragments with 1 cm radius.
Sample 7, Roof thatch	*Salix* or *Populus*	Similar in appearance to *Salix* or *Populus* in Sample 2.

a. Charcoal identified by Terah L. Smiley.
b. Wood identified by C. Wes Ferguson and R. A. Wright.

study area and at sheet erosion site Arizona EE:2:41. Several Tanque Verde Red-on-brown sherds were collected from Unit 2 near Section MC–7 in the west bank of Cienega Creek, upstream from the junction with Matty Wash.

Ridge Sites

Late ceramic sites of the Rincon and Tanque Verde phases were frequently found on surrounding ridges that adjoined the floodplain of Cienega Creek (Fig. 1.3). Village habitation was on ridge crests (eroded terraces), as well as on tips of ridges near the junction of small tributary drainages. In general, the cultural deposits were shallow and lacked an alluvial covering.

Buried Historic Remains

According to Fred Barnett in 1957, adobe corrals and structures identified with the Sanford Ranch could be found near the junction of Matty Wash and Cienega Creek. The remains of only one historic building, designated Arizona EE:2:38, were associated with the terminal alluvial events—Units 1 and 2. The rock floor of this structure was built on the Sanford formation before the deposition of the overlying Unit 1. The recent cutting of the arroyo of Cienega Creek has partly destroyed the floor. Near this structure in the Sanford formation, fragments of a historic green glass beer bottle were found, along with pieces of

Figure 2.7. Early Pioneer period pit house exposed in the east bank of Matty Wash at Arizona EE:2:10. The pit house is indicated by the recessed cut in the bank.

Figure 2.8. Colonial period pit house in the east bank of Matty Wash at Arizona EE:2:34. The gravel lens at the rear of the excavation marks a local erosion surface ("S") from which the floor of the pit house was originally dug.

TABLE 2.2
Mammal Bones from Arizona EE:2:30

Species*	Number of Bones
ARTIODACTYLA	
Cervus sp., elk	4
Odocoileus hemionus, mule deer	55
Odocoileus virginianus, white-tailed deer	9
Odocoileus sp., deer	15
Antilocapra americana, pronghorn	31
cf *Ovis canadensis*, bighorn sheep	3
LAGOMORPHA	
Lepus californicus, black-tailed jackrabbit	1
Lepus sp., jackrabbit	24
Sylvilagus sp., cottontail	2
RODENTIA	
Thomomys sp., pocket gopher	1
Rodent, no further identification	1
CARNIVORA	
Lynx rufus, bobcat	4
Canis latrans, coyote	2
Canis familiaris, domestic dog	Articulated skeleton

*Identified by W. J. Schaldach, Jr., and J. J. Hester.

metal. Bones of domestic livestock (burro and goat) have also been found in the Sanford formation near the corral (Fig. 1.3).

COCHISE CULTURE

A nearly continuous late preceramic and ceramic cultural sequence is present in the Cienega Valley (Fig. 2.16). The preceramic occupation is identified as the San Pedro stage of the Cochise culture, reported from southeastern Arizona by Sayles and Antevs (1941) and by Sayles (1983).

San Pedro Stage

Three preceramic sites were assigned to the San Pedro stage of the Cochise culture. Two of these, Arizona EE:2:12 and EE:2:35, were studied by digging cooking pits and tools from the vertical arroyo walls located along Cienega Creek and in the lower reach of Matty Wash. The limited amount of artifactual data recovered from these excavations was briefly outlined above (see *Preceramic Sites*). More extensive investigations at site Arizona EE:2:30, located on the upper reach of Matty Wash (see Fig. 1.3), are described below.

Excavations

Testing at Arizona EE:2:30 consisted of three excavated pits. Tests 1 and 2 were dug by Emil Haury and his seminar students in 1955, and Frank Eddy used hired labor to dig Test 3 in 1957. These excavations revealed a thick midden stratigraphically positioned at the contact of Units 3 and 100 (see Fig. 1.6). The cultural deposit likely reflected the trash accumulation of a San Pedro stage base camp occupied over many years on a seasonal basis (Eddy 1958). Associated with the midden accumulation were 22 pits; 19 of them were classified (in order of frequency) as: undercut, straight-sided, and types with flared rims. The undercut, or bell-shaped, pit was similar to the pits at the San Pedro stage type site, Benson:5:10 (Gila Pueblo survey; Sayles and Antevs 1941, fig. 9). Straight-sided pits may represent a form adapted to digging in a loose midden where the material had a tendency to cave easily. Two large pits with flared rims, thought to be pit houses, contained additional small, internal, subfloor pits.

On the basis of fill, both undercut and straight-sided pits were interpreted as cooking pits. Five of the cooking pits had marked charcoal concentrations in the lower third of the structure (Table 2.1), with associated fragments of mammal bone (Table 2.2) and clusterings of basalt hearthstones. An ethnographic analogy may be drawn from Opler's (1941: 357, 367) description of the mescal pits of the Chiricahua Apache.

Pit 14 was of unusual interest because of its shape and contents (Fig. 2.9). The undercut pit contained two superimposed layers of hearthstones and charcoal separated by layers of sterile sand. A subfloor gutter encircled the floor perimeter. The pit contents reflected the practice of sequential cookings of plant and animal foodstuffs by hearthstone baking. The sand layers not only raised the level of the oven floor but also increased the heat retention qualities of the hearth rocks.

Pits containing fill lacking charcoal or hearthstones were interpreted as storage bins. Although only two pits fit this description, it is quite possible that many of the pits filled with trash and burials were originally used for storage.

One large pit with a flared rim and an internal subsurface storage bin was partially exposed during a trenching operation. Because of its size, more than 1.4 m wide and over 0.45 m deep, it was tentatively interpreted as a pit house (following Sayles 1945, fig. 2), but post holes, fire basin, and entryway were lacking in the structure. A second possible pit house was discovered in the floor of Test 3, as illustrated in the southwest corner of the excavations shown in Figure 2.4.

In addition to the deep cooking pits, many surface hearths with attributes fitting the pattern described at Benson:5:10 were exposed in the midden. These surface hearths consisted of thermally-fractured basalt hearthstones and charcoal concentrated in shallow depressions in the midden.

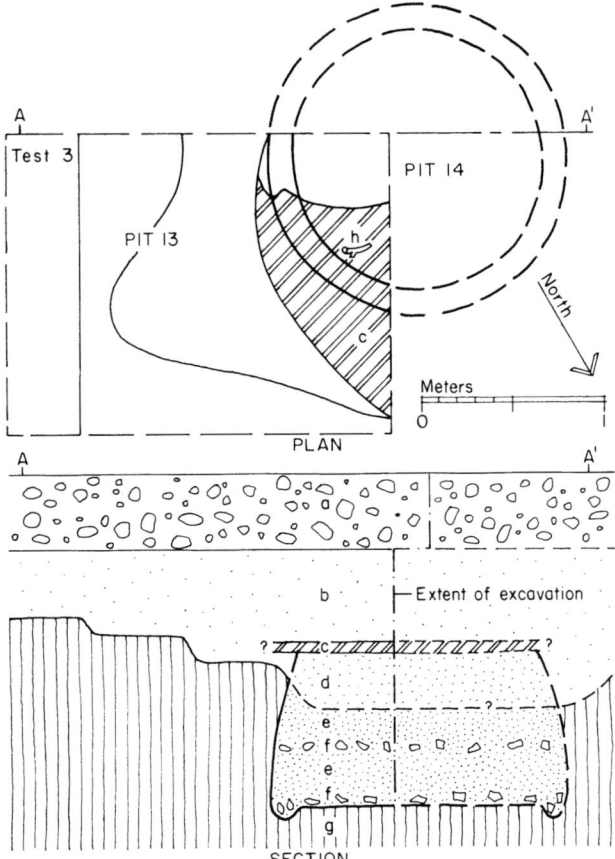

Figure 2.9. Plan and section of superimposed pits at Arizona EE:2:30: *a*, sand and gravel drift on the Matty Wash arroyo floor; *b*, midden accumulation; *c*, mixed clay and trash, possibly an artificial floor covering Pit 14 fill; *d*, mixed trash and sand; *e*, sterile sand; *f*, mixed sandy clay, charcoal, and hearthstones; *g*, Unit 100; *h*, elk antler found in situ in upper *f* layer.

Likely hearth rock was heated here to be transferred to the deep pit ovens for fireless baking of food stuffs, a consideration supported by the lack of burned oxidation of the earth walls of the deep pit ovens.

Artifacts

Test excavation at Arizona EE:2:30 produced over 140 stone tools. When compared to other preceramic sites, this sample securely dates the midden occupation of Arizona EE:2:30 to the San Pedro stage (Table 2.3).

Ground Stone. A variety of pecked and ground stone tools was recovered from pits and the trash midden. Handstones of both the uniface and biface type were common, and both unshaped and shaped forms were recovered from excavations. The unshaped handstones are natural stream cobbles without perimeter modification (Fig. 2.10 *a*). In contrast, the shaped handstones were edge modified by pecking (Fig. 2.10 *c*). They may have been secondarily used as pounding stones to break up nuts, berries, and grass seeds in preparation for grinding on nether milling stones.

In general, the two working surfaces of bifacial handstones are parallel, although in a few cases these grinding facets converge, giving the tool a wedge-shaped profile that may indicate extreme tool wear. Sayles (Sayles and Antevs 1941, pl. 15 *c*) considered this wedged tool shape diagnostic of the San Pedro tool assemblage.

Although some of the handstones are large, most of them are easily manipulated with one hand in a grinding motion. The shape of the oval working surface of the milling stone indicates a reciprocal arc-shaped motion was used in pulverizing food and materials. The granite and vesicular basalt tools were suitable for rough grinding of bulky products, whereas the fine-grained basalt and sandstone tools were better adapted for finer grinding and pulverizing such as making meal from grass seeds.

The protopestles (Fig. 2.10 *b*) are elongated and semirectangular, and they were completely shaped by pecking and grinding.

The milling stones were modified by edge pecking, and the important interior face was pecked into a deep or shallow oval-shaped basin. The oval shape restricted the handstone grinding to a reciprocal motion.

A small slab grinding stone (Fig. 2.11 *a*) with two working surfaces was recovered. The grinding surfaces have a series of parallel striae indicating an axial grinding motion. The waterworn slab of granite is small and it may have been held on the lap when in use.

Thin, disk-shaped pecking stones exhibit perimeters battered by use. One example is pitted in the side, perhaps to ensure a better grip.

Pebble hammerstones (Fig. 2.12 *m*) made from natural round cobbles also exhibit numerous battered edges from use (Haury 1950: 256). These hammer tools were used in the manufacture of flaked stone tools and in shaping and resharpening the milling implements.

Small disks (Fig. 2.11 *b*) with biconical perforations, doughnutlike in appearance, may represent forerunners of the stone rings that occur among the later Hohokam. Di Peso (1956: 437) has given a fertility interpretation to similar objects. A large, thick unperforated disk (Fig. 2.11 *c*) of red granite was also recovered. The sides of the disk are parallel and lack the convexity of handstones. A small, circular depression occurs in the center of one side. Sayles suggested that this disk may have been a blank for a stone bowl.

A small cruciform object of red jasper was removed from the midden exposure by Harry Barnett. Shaped by pecking and grinding and then highly polished, the stone was fashioned in a symmetrical cross form with the ends of the arms neatly squared. Sayles (Sayles and Antevs 1941, pl. 15 *b*) depicted a similarly shaped object from Benson:5:10, indicating it was a rubbing stone. Evidence of abrasion between the cross arms of the object from Arizona EE:2:30 is lacking, and therefore it was probably an ornament. Similarly, Haury (1950: 304) interpreted several pressure-chipped crosses from the San Pedro levels in Ventana Cave as amulets.

Several elongated, trapezoidal objects (Fig. 2.12 *e*) made of thin pieces of tabular stone were recovered from the midden. They differ little from other similar unmodified pieces of material except for grinding on the edges and corners. These artifacts could have been suspended from a thong and worn around the neck as pendants.

TABLE 2.3
San Pedro Stage Stone Tool Complexes from Cienega Valley Compared with Complexes from Adjacent Regions

Tools	Ventana Cave Levels 3–5 Haury (1950)	Cochise Culture Southeastern Ariz. Sayles and Antevs (1941)	Cienega Valley	
			Arizona EE:2:30	Surveyed Sites
Handstones				
Uniface	P	P	P	AZ EE:2:12, 2:13
Biface	P	P	P	AZ EE:2:12, 2:13
Pestles	P	P	P	A
Millingstones				
Deep basin	P	P	P	A
Shallow basin	A	P	P	AZ EE:2:12, 2:35
Slab	P	P	P	AZ EE:2:12
Mortars	A	P	A	A
Planes	P	P	P	A
Scrapers				
Side	P	P	P	AZ EE:2:12
End	P	P	P	A
Hollow	P	P	A	A
Discoidal	P	P	P	A
Choppers	P	A	A	A
Gravers	P	A	A	A
Drills	P	A	A	A
Projectile points	P	P	P	AZ EE:2:12
Blades	P	P	P	AZ EE:2:13

P, present; A, absent.

Figure 2.10. Handstones from Arizona EE:2:30: *a*, unshaped; *b*, protopestle; *c*, shaped. Length of *a* is 12 cm.

Figure 2.11. Ground stone tools from Arizona EE:2:30: *a*, small slab grinding stone; *b*, perforated disk fragment; *c*, unperforated disk. Length of *b* is 9.7 cm.

Figure 2.12. Chipped and ground stone tools from Arizona EE:2:30: *a*, *b*, triangular blades; *c*, *d*, stemmed points; *e*, pendant; *f*, thin bifacial disk; *g*, keeled endscraper; *h*, round-nosed endscraper; *i*, elongate keeled sidescraper; *j*, thick bifacial disk; *k*, rough flake sidescraper; *l*, plane; *m*, pebble hammerstone; *n*, thick discoidal scraper. Length of *a* is 5.5 cm.

Chipped Stone. Chipped stone artifacts equal about 48 percent of the total tool assemblage. The tools from Arizona EE:2:30 that were manufactured by percussion, as well as most of the pressure-chipped artifacts, were made with fine-grained basalt. Exceptions include the finely chipped stemmed points fashioned from chalcedony. The technological inferiority of most of the cutting tools may be partially attributed to the poor conchoidal fracturing quality of the basalt. The source of this material is unknown. The only bedrock outcroppings in the immediate vicinity are highly metamorphic mudstones of Cretaceous age that would be unsuitable for stone knapping. Igneous outcroppings in the nearby mountains were probably visited by people of the Cochise culture.

Several planes were recovered from the midden. A plane (Fig. 2.12 *l*) is defined as a core or thick flake tool characterized by a pronounced plano-convex profile, steep-sided cutting edge, and round or elongate outline (Haury 1950: 207). It is apparently produced by developing a striking platform on a natural cobble. The steeply chipped cutting edge is made by right angle blows on this surface, resulting in a domed, convex top. The original striking platform becomes the tool base. The top forms a convenient handle for an axial or push-pull work motion, with the base held nearly parallel to the material being planed. The cutting edge is occasionally outflaring and extends around the tool's perimeter; it often shows evidence of use by its battered appearance. The outflaring nature of this edge gives the tool an inverted bell-shaped cross section.

Although the term 'planer' for this artifact type infers its use in woodworking and hide scraping, it is also thought to have been used to remove pulp matter from the fibrous leaves of cacti. According to Sayles, this interpreted use as a pulping plane is based on the form of the artifact and its frequent occurrence in preceramic sites whose distributions correlate with the agave, yucca, and related types of cacti that provided cordage used by natives of the Southwest. Haury (1950: 209) found planes were strongly diagnostic of the gathering-hunting peoples of Ventana Cave during preceramic times.

A flake tool produced by working on only one face results in a plano-convex form called a scraper. The cutting edge is usually inclined at a low angle, although the snub-nosed scraper forms tend toward the steep angle of the planer. Because there is considerable variation in the types and placement of the cutting edge, it is one of the diagnostic features in subtyping a collection (Haury 1950: 212).

The sidescrapers recovered from Arizona EE:2:30 are of the rough flake and elongate varieties. The rough flake (Fig. 2.12 *k*) category was originally established as a catchall grouping for the Ventana Cave material, and it included bulky scrapers with rough chipping (Haury 1950: 217). The jagged working edge, produced by percussion, is largely confined to one portion of the thick flake. The elongate sidescrapers (Fig. 2.12 *i*) were made from thin flakes and have a long oval outline. Chipping extended almost entirely around the tool perimeter. One example was keeled, but another lacked this feature.

Endscrapers are distinctive with retouch placed on the end of the long axis of a flake rather than along its sides. Retouching in both positions suggests a dual use for the tool (Haury 1950: 224–225). Both keeled and round-nosed endscrapers were recovered from Arizona EE:2:30. The central ridge of the upper surface of the keeled endscraper (Fig. 2.12 *g*) is pronounced, and the steeply inclined working edge approached the angle of the previously described plane (Haury 1950: 227). The round-nosed scraper (Fig. 2.12 *h*) is an elongate flake tool lacking a pronounced central ridge, but having a steep snub-nosed cutting edge. The examples from Arizona EE:2:30 lack the forward hump on the convex surface noted by Haury (1950: 227).

The discoidal scrapers (Fig. 2.12 *n*) generally fit Haury's (1950: 232) thin flake subtype, described as plano-convex in cross section. The tools from the site tend toward a convex keel shape and a steep working face that may be snub-nosed in places on the retouched cutting edge. This working edge generally extends around the perimeter of the tool.

More than 268 thin waste chips with fine, serrate, retouched edges were found in the trash and pits. These chips have no consistent form, and they vary from small to large flakes (Haury 1950: 236). They may represent the use of waste materials in cutting and scraping activities. Many of the forms probably equate with Haury's (1950: 213) class of "thin flake side serrated." Because they probably do not represent an intentionally-fashioned tool form, they were not included in the tabulation and analysis of tool types.

Among the artifacts from Arizona EE:2:30 with bifacial cutting edges were projectile points (Fig. 2.12 *c*, *d*) and blanks. The thin flake points were developed by pressure chipping from an essentially triangular blank with a straight or convex base and slightly convex sides. Notching produced a parallel-sided stem. Tangs were both sharp and rounded, and projected either laterally or obliquely (Haury 1950, fig. 50). All the points were small and suitable for arrow or dart hafting, drills, and secondary use as cutting edges. The points from the midden at Arizona EE:2:30 differ from those illustrated by Sayles and Antevs (1941, pl. 16 *c*, *d*) in that they are smaller, thinner, and lack the pronounced expanding-base stem. Triangular blades or blanks (Fig. 2.12 *a*, *b*) compare closely with types previously defined by Sayles (Sayles and Antevs 1941, pl 16 *f*) for the San Pedro stage.

A small, thin disk (Fig. 2.12 *f*) found at the site is similar to a disk type described by Sayles (Sayles and Antevs 1941, pl. 16 *e*) as a distinctive trait of the San Pedro complex. Examples from the midden and pits include forms that are flaked all over and those modified only on the tool perimeter. This artifact may have been used as a sidescraper. Thick disks (Fig. 2.12 *j*) were produced by chipping on both faces of a core or large flake, producing a sinuous edge around the entire perimeter of the tool. Most examples have secondary retouching on this edge. The bifacial spalls reported by Sayles (Sayles and Antevs 1941, pl. 16 *b*) for the San Pedro stage are similar.

In summary, the stone tool complex of Arizona EE:2:30 would have satisfied the requirements of a small group of people in a desert environment who lived by hunting and gathering. Sayles (Sayles and Antevs 1941: 28) stressed the importance of the shift in relative proportion of ground to chipped stone tools in the developmental sequence of the Cochise culture. It was suggested that a major portion of the Sulphur Spring stage subsistence economy was based on plant gathering activities as reflected in the predominance of ground over chipped stone tools. As the Cochise tradition developed, this ratio was reversed, a trend reflected at Arizona EE:2:30 with a ratio of approximately 52 percent ground stone tools to 48 percent chipped stone tools. These figures, however, have significance only when compared to the development that preceded them. Taken as an indicator of the relative proportion of the economy focused on either hunting or gathering, these percentages would seem to indicate a near balance in subsistence pursuits.

Bone. Both whole and split bone awls were recovered from the excavations. The only whole bone awl (Fig. 2.13 d) in the collection was made from a deer ulna; it has a ground end and a high polish from use. Its shape and wear suggest that it may have been used as a punch or reamer, perhaps in leather working.

Split bone awls (Fig. 2.13 a, b) were produced by splitting mammal long bone shafts lengthwise. The tapered working ends were ground and polished from wear. On several unclassified tips and shafts, wear and polishing indicate that the bone pieces were used, but the fragmentary nature of the specimens hampered a more detailed classification.

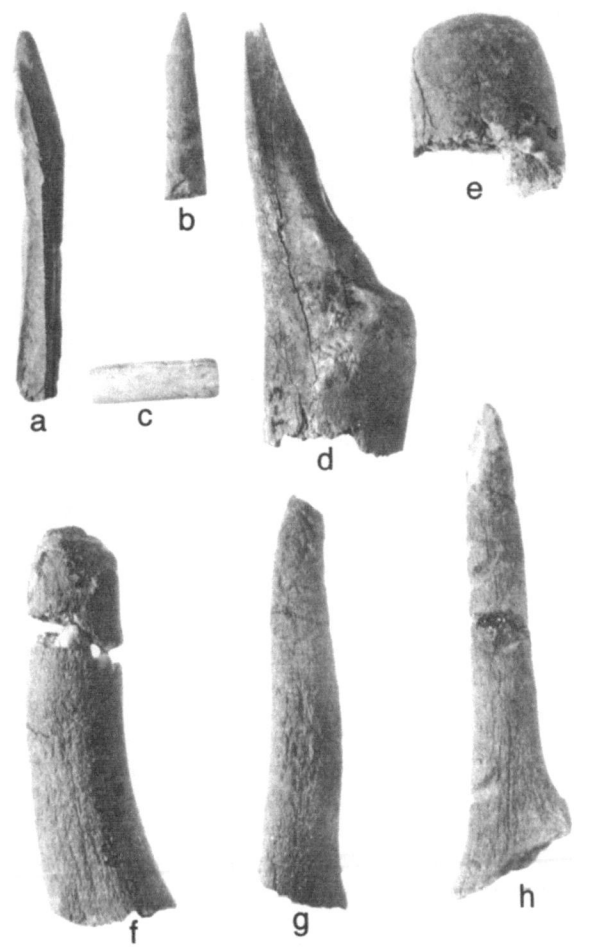

Figure 2.13. Bone tools from Arizona EE:2:30: a, b, split bone awls; c, polished cylinder; d, whole bone awl; e, hammer; f–h, tine flakers. Length of c is 3.1 cm.

One end of a section of antler was bluntly rounded off by cutting and grinding. Haury (1950: 384) described a similar type of implement and suggested it could have been used as a hammer. It may also have been a tool handle, with the recovered portion representing the butt end of the grip (Fig. 2.13 e).

One example of a mammal leg bone tube, similar to an artifact described by Haury (1950: 381), was found at Arizona EE:2:30. The fragment has a beveled edge that was formed by cutting and grinding.

A small, ground, and well-polished bone cylinder (Fig. 2.13 c) with a conical hole drilled at one end was removed from the midden. This piece may have been used as a handle on a small shaft.

Several deer antler tine flakers were also recovered. They were apparently used without intentional modification for the pressure chipping of stone. Evidence of use is observed in the form of the blunted and scarred tips, and some of the cuts extend well down the tine shaft toward the handle grips (Fig. 2.13 f–h).

In contrast to the stone tool complex, which was interpreted as functioning largely in the preparation of food, the bone and antler tool industry appears to have been developed for processing other materials. Although some of the tools were used in stone flaking, probably the principal use of bone awls was in the treatment of hides, a material that may have been used for containers and clothing even though articles of this nature were not preserved in the archaeological record.

Burials

Evidence of eight San Pedro burials was found in pits associated with the midden. The difficulty of extraction from the compacted fill and the fragmentary nature of the specimens because of exposure and erosion precluded any possibility of an osteological study, but a few distributional comments may be made.

There was an apparent clustering of burials in one restricted portion of the midden area. Seven burials were recovered from a series of four pits immediately adjacent to one another, and in three cases actual intersecting indicated successive construction. Burials were found in all three types of pits—undercut, straight-sided, and pits with flared rims—indicating a secondary use of all three kinds for inhumation. Three pits with flared rims contained pairs of burials, which may indicate that their primary function was inhumation. The second burial of a pair in one of these pits was intrusive. The pit of the original burial contained a gravel fill that was unmixed with organic debris, perhaps representing the collection of gravel from a nearby drainage bed specifically for the purpose of covering the deceased. It may also indicate that the pit had been previously dug and utilized for other purposes such as storage.

Body orientation was determined in four cases. Three of the skeletons were lying on their sides, two on the right side and one on the left. In the fourth instance, the skull was oriented upright, but this burial was probably disturbed by the intrusion of one of the other burials. Three of the bodies were facing south and the fourth faced north. The only complete skeleton lay on its right side in a flexed position with the hands crossed and brought up in front of the face.

In all cases, burial offerings were lacking, but the possibility exists that perishable items were placed with the body at the time of inhumation.

The articulated skeleton of a young dog (*Canis familiaris*) was found near the top of the main midden in Test 1 against the west arroyo bank of Matty Wash (Fig. 2.3). Because of the articulated nature of the skeleton, this find may represent the intentional burial of a camp pet or hunting companion. If the animal had been used for food, certainly the skeletal frame would have been dismembered during the butchering process (Table 2.2).

Discussion

Based on the tool complex and undercut pit features, the preceramic occupation at Arizona EE:2:30 was culturally identified with the broad pattern of the San Pedro stage of the Cochise culture. The numerous pit features at the site revealed that the various forms were used for storage, burial, house, and cooking functions. Generally debris accumulates laterally, and the vertical growth of this midden was unusual in an open campsite. This vertical growth indicated a more stable settlement such as might be found among a group that periodically returned to a semipermanent base camp at intervals in the seasonal round of hunting and gathering. A more stable settlement is not usually associated with an economy based solely on hunting, but on one in which gathering also plays a part. The balance in subsistence activities could have been achieved through the availability of both a wide range of easily accessible life zones and the even more convenient local cienegas (mainly of Units 4 and 6) that must have held an abundant amount of wild aquatic foods. The presence of corn pollen from contemporary sediments in the area also suggests a third component to the diet (Fig. 2.16), and perhaps incipient agriculture.

The preceramic survey sites were characterized by a scantiness of cultural debris and the presence of surface and deep hearths. Overall these exposures appeared to be highly temporary campsites where small groups halted to exploit the local food resources on a seasonal basis. The waste chips, the minimum number of portable shaped tools, and the general lack of concentrated trash supported this interpretation. Perhaps they were special-activity sites for hunting and plant gathering used by peoples ranging out of a base camp like that at Arizona EE:2:30.

A study of the Great Basin Shoshonean Indians by Steward (1955: 101) provides an interesting ethnographic parallel for the socioeconomic interpretation of the San Pedro stage archaeological data from Arizona EE:2:30 and the other preceramic survey sites. Steward's analysis of early contact Shoshonean society stresses the twin limiting features of the sparse, erratic desert environment and the simple level of the hunting and gathering technology. Of particular importance was the effect of wild vegetable products in influencing separatism (as opposed to interfamily cooperation) in exploitative activities. Families were widely scattered about the countryside when engaged in collecting activities, thus effecting an even take of plant products. A concentration of families in a given area would quickly exhaust the limited food supply and create a hardship for the whole group.

Exceptions to this dispersed settlement pattern came about during winter encampments, which were determined by caches of surplus pinyon nuts and which occurred at times when collective hunts could be organized (Steward 1955: 109). Among the animals hunted profitably by collective effort are rabbits and antelope. These animals build up concentrated populations large enough to support groups of families assembled for cooperative hunts. Hunting techniques include surrounding or driving the animals into nets and corrals. Other opportunities for larger aggregates of people to get together for a limited time include fish runs and concentrations of waterfowl in marsh areas.

The environmental features and material culture of the San Pedro stage parallel those discussed by Steward (1955: 101) for the Shoshone. Projecting the ethnographic analogy into the past, the reconstructed picture is one of a nomadic subsistence cycle. Paralleling the Shoshonean winter encampment, the Cochise people found a sufficient and concentrated food supply to permit assembly for part of each year at base camps of the kind illustrated by the midden occupation at Arizona EE:2:30. Here, a macroband of families could have collectively hunted the large rabbit population and the herds of antelope. Collecting activities might have been centered on plant foods from the nearby cienegas (chiefly of alluvial Units 4 and 6) and the local grasses. Other assembly occasions may have been in the spring and summer when small gardens of corn were planted, tended, and harvested. Any surplus crop could have been stored in the deep pits dug into the midden area and within the semipermanent houses.

During the fall, individual families may have been induced to break away from the band to carry out separate collecting activities at the small fly camps such as Arizona EE:2:12 and EE:2:35. Additional trips to the nearby mountains may have been made to harvest other plant foods and hunt mammals such as whitetail deer, big horn sheep(?), and elk, which frequent the higher altitudes. Thus, a desert culture, as defined by Jennings (1957) for the western United States, is indicated for these people.

HOHOKAM CULTURE

The ceramic cultural sequence is presented within a framework of phases forming the Tucson Hohokam cultural tradition defined by Kelly (1938, 1978) at the Hodges Ruin near Tucson. Tuthill (1947: 17) correlated Kelly's phase units with his work at the Tres Alamos site in the San Pedro Valley and the Gila River Basin Hohokam sequence (Fig. 2.16). In general, the Hohokam sequence in Cienega Valley corresponds with the Gila River Basin Hohokam sequence established through Gila Pueblo's excavation of Snaketown (Gladwin and others 1937) and reaffirmed through the work of the Arizona State Museum during 1964 and 1965 (Haury 1976).

Vahki-Estrella Phase

Early Pioneer period occupation was demonstrated by a buried pit house of Vahki-Estrella age at Arizona EE:2:10 (Fig. 2.7). The phase identification was based on the occurrence of micaceous-tempered Vahki plain and red wares,

TABLE 2.4
Occurrence of Ceramics on Sites in Cienega Valley

Phases and Dates	Ceramics	Sites Arizona EE:2:												
		10	40	14	42	34	30	36	11	32	37	41	43	45
Tucson A.D. 1300–1400 or 1500	Gila Polychrome													D
	Tanque Verde Red-on-brown													D
	Tanque Verde Polychrome													P
	Red Ware													P
	Plain Ware													P
	Santa Cruz Polychrome													T
	Babocomari Polychrome					T								T
Tanque Verde A.D. 1200–1300	Tanque Verde Red-on-brown			D	P	P			P	D	P	D	D	D
	Red Ware			P	P				P	P	P	P	P	P
	Plain Ware			P	P				P	P	P	P	P	P
	Corrugated Ware					P						P	P	P
Rincon A.D. 900–1200	Rincon Red-on-brown	D	P					P	D	D	P	P		
	Red Ware	P	P						P	P	P	P		
	Plain Ware	P	P					P	P	P	P	P		
	Dragoon Red-on-brown					T				T				
	Mimbres Black-on-white												T	
	Roosevelt Black-on-white												T	
Rillito– Cañada del Oro A.D. 600–900	Rillito-Cañada del Oro Red-on-brown					D								
	Red Ware					P	P							
	Plain Ware					P	P							
	Gila Butte Red-on-buff					T								
Cañada del Oro A.D. 600–700	Red Ware					P								
	Plain Ware					P								
	Gila Butte Red-on-buff					T								
Snaketown A.D. 400–600	Snaketown Grooved		P											
	Pioneer Painted		P											
	Plain Ware		P											
Vahki–Estrella A.D. 1–300	Estrella Grooved	P												
	Vahki Red	P												
	Vahki Plain	P												

P, present; D, dominant painted type; T, trade ware.

the presence of one Estrella grooved sherd, and the absence of painted pottery (Table 2.4). Unfortunately, the small number of sherds recovered (32) allowed only a tentative phase placement.

The pit house measured 3.4 m wide with an average depth of 75 cm. The walls were slightly undercut and the floor sloped toward the deep end of the house on the south side. The walls and floor were unplastered, consisting of the rough surface of the pit excavation into Unit 100. No additional architectural features were uncovered.

A small quantity of tools was removed from the pit house fill and the hearth on the immediately adjacent surface. It is significant that the tool types differed little from the ground stone assemblage described at the San Pedro site at Arizona EE:2:30.

A basin milling stone from the hearth, along with the handstones from the house, indicated a continued dependence on wild food products. Whether or not much agriculture had entered the scene is debatable. The several flake knives, sidescrapers, and hammerstones recovered were of little diagnostic value, because they have a wide distribution in time.

If the large, deep pit interpreted as a house at Arizona EE:2:30 and the milling stone complex are compared to the pit house at Arizona EE:2:10, the major cultural difference is the addition of pottery to the material culture inventory. Otherwise, the archaeological remains and the stratigraphic situation suggest a direct cultural continuity.

Snaketown Phase

The Snaketown phase was represented by a single trash mound area (Arizona EE:2:40) on the end of a low ridge that rose slightly above the floodplain of Cienega Creek (see Fig. 1.3). The cultural identification was made on the basis of plain wares that equated with Pioneer period types. Similarity was noted in the thinness of the ceramics and the lack of red wares. There was a decrease in the amount of micaceous temper compared to that found in Vahki plain ware. The presence of a single Snaketown grooved sherd supported this placement (Table 2.4).

No visible signs of architecture were observed, but occurrence of trash mounds indicated an occupation of some permanency—possibly some form of village habitation.

Cañada del Oro Phase

A sheet erosion site, Arizona EE:2:14, produced a ceramic complex consisting of a micaceous and sand grit tempered plain ware associated with a small amount of plain red ware (Table 2.4). Painted wares occurring in the greatest frequency were intrusive Gila Butte Red-on-buff sherds, derived from the Gila and Salt river valleys occupied by the River Hohokam. The intrusive sherds placed this site in the early Colonial period. Lithic material was extremely scarce and not directly attributable to this phase of occupation.

Undifferentiated Cañada del Oro-Rillito Phase

Two sites were assigned a combined Cañada del Oro-Rillito phase designation because it was not possible to separate the painted wares by phase at Arizona EE:2:42 and diagnostic painted sherds were lacking at Arizona EE:2:34.

Arizona EE:2:42 was a sheet trash zone lying on the tip of a ridge projection above the junction of two small tributaries of Matty Wash (see Fig. 1.3). Undated pottery included polished and unpolished plain and red wares. Although later Tanque Verde phase material was present, the major occupation was represented by red-on-brown ceramics that occur mainly in Cañada del Oro-Rillito phases. One intrusive Gila Butte Red-on-buff sherd was collected. On the basis of the buff paste, it was probably derived from the Gila-Salt drainage area through trade. There was no evidence of tools.

Arizona EE:2:34, the other site assigned to this undifferentiated phase category, consisted of a buried pit house. The subsurface part of the house was a deep, rectangular, adobe-plastered pit with rounded corners and sloping or battered walls (Fig. 2.14; see also Fig. 2.8). The dimensions of the pit house were 4.65 m by about 3.15 m.

An entryway 1.9 m long was located in the middle of the east wall. Exit from the house was made by a step up into this passage. A second step led from the entryway onto the old ground surface ("S"). The entrance passage was nearly horizontal, with a slight depression near its outer end that may have served as a water-catching basin. In plan view (Fig. 2.14 a), the entry had a bulbous shape that expanded at the end of the house from a narrow door measuring 50 cm to a maximum width of 75 cm near the exit. In cross section (Fig. 2.14 c), the excavated part of the entry had rounded walls.

Two slots occurred toward the house end of the entry. One of the slots, immediately above the house step-up, contained a fragment of a burned ash branch that may have served as a step rung. The second slot lacked evidence of charcoal and was filled with clean sand. A similar type of depression occurring in house ramps was interpreted by Di Peso (1956, fig. 15) as a deflector slot.

The intact portion of the floor had a number of interesting features. Two deep post holes occurred toward the remaining corners of the house; one contained the charred butt of a major support for the roof. These post holes were probably paralleled by two others that since then have been eroded away by arroyo cutting. Two shallow depressions marked points where secondary braces may have been propped to support the roof cross members. Additional floor features

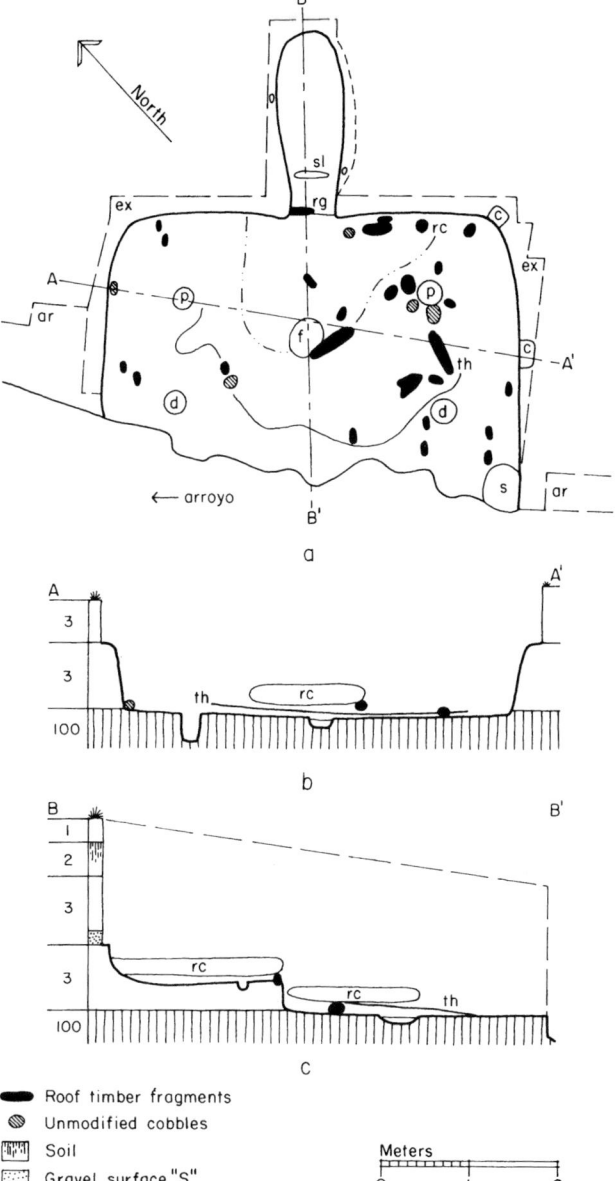

Figure 2.14. Pit house excavated at Arizona EE:2:34: *a*, plan; *b*, *c*, sections (alluvial designations are indicated in the columns at left). Key: *f*, fire pit; *p*, post holes; *d*, shallow depressions; *s*, subfloor pit; *sl*, slot in entryway; *rg*, rung set in entry floor; *c*, coping of plastered wall over old surface; *th*, thatch roof matting; *rc*, roofing clay; *ar*, "faced-up" arroyo wall; *ex*, extent of excavation.

included a shallow-basin fire pit filled with fine white ash and a plastered-over subfloor pit in the southwestern corner of the room.

The 30 cm floor layer fill contained quantities of burned roofing material. Fragments of charred poles 10 cm to 15 cm in diameter lay on or near the floor and were generally oriented parallel to the short axis of the house. These burned timbers undoubtedly represented the remains of the roof cross members; ash, willow or poplar, Western yellow pine(?), and juniper were used (Table 2.1). A layer of charred grass, cane, and bark thatch, 7.0 cm to 8.0 cm thick, was distributed over the central portion of the room. This material lay directly on the floor in the southern part of the pit but was underlain by as much as 10 cm of sterile alluvium in the northern half. Overlying the thatch was a 10 cm to 15 cm layer of hard clay that in places had been oxidized by fire to a light orange color. Five water-worn cobbles completed the inventory of material associated with the roof fall.

To reconstruct the roof, four major upright supports were capped with cross beams. These in turn were additionally supported by two props butted in shallow depressions on the house floor. Lighter stringers leaned from the ground surface to the central frame. This skeleton construction was covered with a layer of thatch and capped with a thick coating of mud plaster. The cobbles found on the floor may have been used as weights to secure tag ends on the roof. Entryway roofing followed this same pattern. From the two small post holes on the old ground surface adjacent to the entry wall, we inferred the bulbous passage had vertical sides. Reed and grass impressions in the entryway also indicated this kind of construction.

Polished and unpolished plain and red ware sherds were recovered from the house and floor fill. The Cañada del Oro or Rillito phase identification was based on the thinness of these sherds and their micaceous temper. Several Tanque Verde Red-on-brown sherds were removed from the overlying alluvial material (Units 1 and 2). The number of lithic tools recovered was extremely small.

Architecturally, this structure showed stronger affinities with the Mogollon culture to the east than with the Hohokam culture, as evidenced by the long lateral entryway, the deep pit nature of the structure, and the use of the pit walls as part of the house itself. Paradoxically, the plain wares indicated that the structure was occupied by the people of the Tucson Hohokam tradition as defined for this portion of the Cienega Valley. However, because this valley lies in a peripheral position to the Tucson area, a certain amount of overlap with adjacent regions may be expected.

Rincon Phase

Sites of Rincon phase occupations were located with nearly equal frequency on both the floodplain (Arizona EE:2:10, 2:14, 2:30, and 2:36) and the adjacent ridges (Arizona EE:2:11, 2:32, and 2:37).

Direct evidence of architecture was present at ridge site Arizona EE:2:11. Rectangular rock alignments measuring 5 m by 1.5 m probably served as bases for jacal-type superstructures. Such structures were scattered at random along the crest of a ridge for a quarter mile (0.4 km). The lack of orientation or clustering suggested a successive seasonal occupation or an open village plan. The presence of small trash mounds on other ridge sites (Arizona EE:2:32 and 2:37) presented the possibility of village occupation, even though architectural evidence was lacking.

The phase assignment was made from indigenous Rincon Red-on-brown sherds. Undecorated pottery included both polished and unpolished plain and red wares. A nearly complete jar (Fig. 2.15 b) recovered in situ from the top of the Unit 3 alluvium at Arizona EE:2:14 has a Gila shoulder,

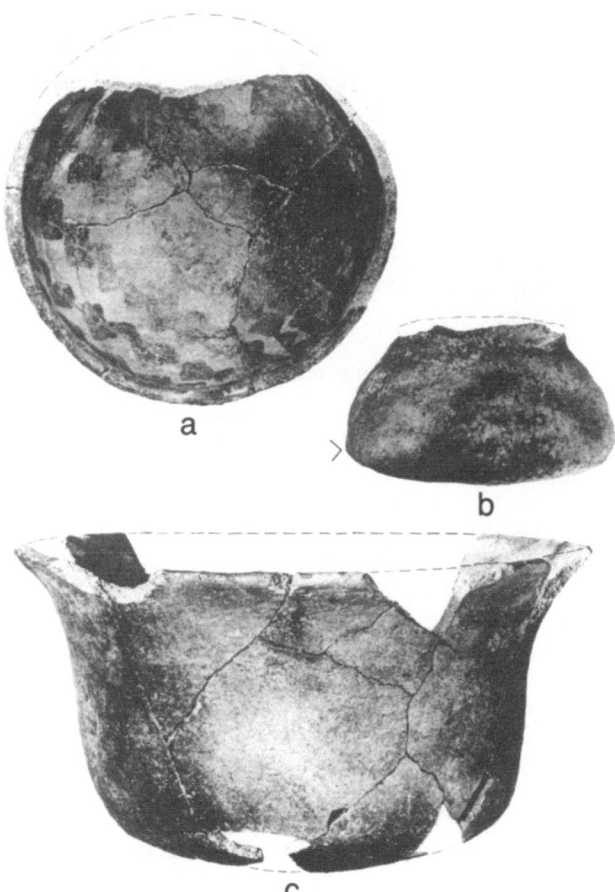

Figure 2.15. Rincon phase ceramic vessels: a, c, red-on-brown bowls from a cremation at Arizona EE:2:10; b, plain ware jar from upper portion of Unit 3 alluvium at Arizona EE:2:14. Diameter of a is 15.2 cm.

characteristic of the corresponding Sacaton phase in the Gila and Salt river valleys. Two restorable bowls (Fig. 2.15 a, c) from the upper trash component at Arizona EE:2:10 were cremation offerings. Red-on-brown design elements plus the flaring form of one of the bowls indicate a Rincon phase pottery identification. Intrusive red-on-brown trade wares were derived from the San Pedro River Valley. Identification of these intrusive types may illustrate a shift in trade relations from the previous exchange linked with the River Hohokam (Table 2.4).

Pecked and ground stone tools collected from Rincon phase sites included troughed metates open at one end, modified unifacial manos with a loaf-shaped cross section, small cobble and large boulder mortars, hammerstones, and one carved stone bowl. Among the chipped stone tools were small expanding base stemmed points, bifacial blades and knives, planes, and several varieties of scrapers. Ornaments included carved shell bracelet fragments and a small slab petroglyph.

The chipped stone assemblage closely resembled tool types of the earlier San Pedro stage of the Cochise culture that were interpreted as hunting and gathering implements. The grinding tools paralleled the types associated with

Hohokam agriculturalists in other parts of the southern desert. The lack of ornamental objects, especially the quantities of carved shell characteristic of the Hohokam elsewhere, is noteworthy.

Settlement during the Rincon phase probably represented a transition from habitation on the floodplain to the adjacent ridges. Surface indications revealed both stable ridge villages and temporary campsites on the floodplain. Ridge sites were usually characterized by sheet or lateral distribution of trash over their surfaces, with the exception of one site that had small, low mounds of rock and trashy soil. On the other hand, lack of organic trash and structures on the floodplain could indicate temporary forms of occupation.

Trade relations presumably were established with people in the adjacent San Pedro Valley as well as with the Gila and Salt valley residents. The tool complex reflected a mixed economy of hunting, gathering, and agriculture.

Because this phase was studied almost entirely from surface collections, it is impossible to make direct associations between the tools, houses, and diagnostic ceramics. In most cases, however, the ceramic evidence shows that occupation that began in the Rincon phase continued into the succeeding Tanque Verde phase with no indication of a break (Table 2.4). Therefore, the subsistence activities outlined probably accurately describe the pattern followed in both cultural time periods.

Tanque Verde Phase

The Tanque Verde phase identification was based on an associated complex of plain, red, and red-on-brown wares. At one site, Arizona EE:2:42, corrugated sherds made with local paste also fit into this trait cluster (Table 2.4). Design elements occurring on Tanque Verde Red-on-brown ceramics represent a regional variation of Tucson area styles. The absence of trade wares was unexpected, but a larger sample of sites might reveal them.

Settlement appeared to be almost entirely on the ridges, and surface indications implied a stable village life. The tool complex, as discussed in the Rincon phase, was indicative of a mixed economy. Because of the small sample, we did not feel the absence of trade wares indicated a lack of outside contact.

Tucson Phase

Tucson phase occupation was represented only at Arizona EE:2:45. The site was on the edge of a low terrace remnant adjoining the floodplain. Surface features included sheet trash and a single depression surrounded by a large ring of stones. The depression was on a hilltop along the southern edge of the site, and probably represented a pit house.

Plain and polished red wares were the predominant pottery types. Local painted wares consisted of nonmicaceous Tanque Verde Red-on-brown and Gila Polychrome, a type usually associated with the Salado migration into southern Arizona. One polychrome sherd showed characteristics described by Danson (1957a: 223) for a variant of Tanque Verde Red-on-brown and two rim sherds from a bowl have similar polychrome decoration. The presence of Babocomari and Santa Cruz polychromes indicated trading and influence from the south. Still earlier Mimbres and Roosevelt black-on-white trade wares revealed a preceding Sedentary period occupation, although these trade wares were not observed elsewhere in the Cienega Valley (Table 2.4).

Deep troughed metates, unifacial loaf-shaped manos, choppers, hammerstones, and a notched stone saw were collected from this site.

DISCUSSION OF THE CULTURAL SEQUENCE

The stratified sequence of sites and their cultural manifestations indicated an essentially continuous prehistoric human occupation in Cienega Valley. The occupation progressed from the preceramic San Pedro stage of the Cochise culture through a sequence of ceramic phases that began with the Vahki-Estrella and continued through the Tucson phase. The ceramic components reported in this study are affiliated with the Hohokam culture of the Tucson area.

The floodplain was mainly used for village and campsite habitation up through the Rillito phase. Thereafter, occupation occurred more frequently on the adjacent ridges. The Rincon phase marked a period of transition to the ridge settlement pattern. In contrast to the early single phase occupation, greater settlement stability occurred, and the villages established during the Rincon phase continued to be occupied in the Tanque Verde phase.

Certain changes and persistences in the tool technology showed that the basic subsistence pattern of the Cienega Creek region from early to late was based on a mixed economy. The ground stone tool complex equated with plant gathering was altered late in the sequence toward an assemblage associated with farming. Specifically, there was a change in the late ceramic horizon from the earlier basin milling stone and handstone to the troughed metate and mano. The continuity of chipped stone tool types equated with hunting and gathering activities illustrated a continued emphasis on these aspects of the economy.

The economy in this region more closely paralleled that of the Desert Hohokam than that of the River Hohokam or San Pedro River Valley areas. Economies in these last two locations were based on irrigation agriculture and elaborate surplus production and exchange systems, whereas the former region was oriented toward subsistence gathering and hunting activities (Di Peso 1953, fig. 31).

The general lack of shell ornaments and other trade goods during most phases must indicate a lack of integration into the more widespread surplus exchange system of the River Hohokam. Nevertheless, the appearance of ceramic trade wares during certain phases (Table 2.4) is regarded as evidence of limited outside contact.

In summary, the prehistoric occupation of Cienega Valley since the time of the San Pedro stage was essentially continuous. Most of the cultural evidence supports the hypothesis of a gradual development of the Hohokam culture from a preceramic Desert Culture base.

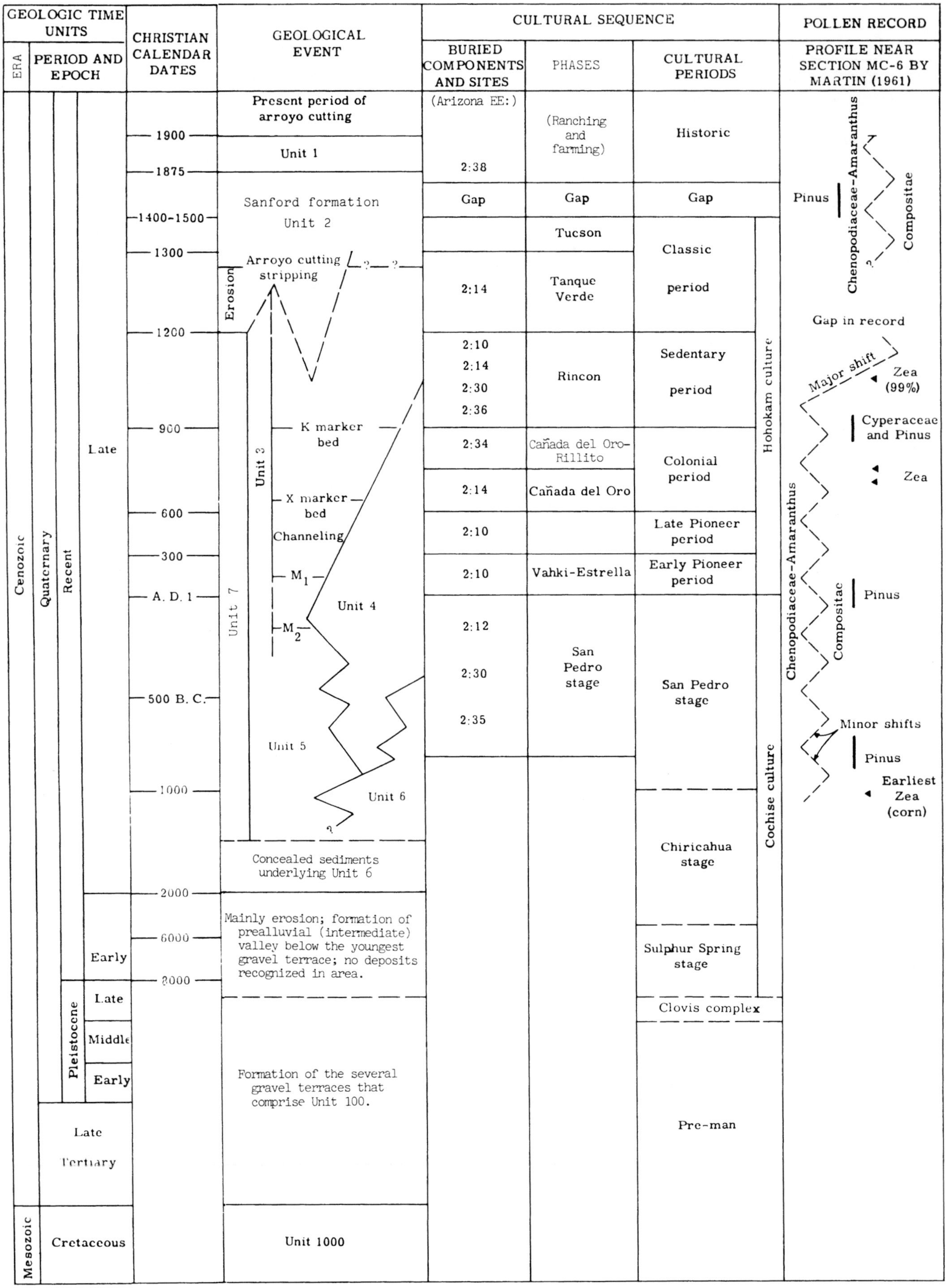

Figure 2.16. Correlation of the geological events, cultural sequence, pollen record, and radiocarbon dates in Cienega Valley.

POLLEN RECORD PROFILE AT SECTION MC-5 BY SCHOENWETTER (1960)	SEDIMENTARY ENVIRONMENT	INFERRED CLIMATIC CONDITIONS	CLIMATIC SUBDIVISIONS (ANTEVS 1955)	APPROXIMATE RADIOCARBON DATE (Years before 1950)	CHRISTIAN CALENDAR DATES
Chenopodiaceae-Amaranthus / Compositae — Major shift — Pinus and Quercus	Arroyo cutting	Unstable wet-dry conditions; rapid precipitation; generally forms a drought; contains short, sharp dry periods.	Neothermal — Medithermal		1900
	Scour-and-fill deposition; fast runoff.				1875
	Formation of a soil zone; fine-grained deposits; slow runoff.	Stable wet conditions; precipitation slow and steady.			1400-1500
					1300
Gap in record — Pinus and Quercus	Arroyo cutting, probably preceded by a period of stripping; fast runoff.	Unstable wet-dry conditions; rapid precipitation; may not have been as intense as the present drought; correlates with the "Great Drought."			1200
	Scour-and-fill deposition; end of deposition in cienegas; fairly fast runoff.	Alternating stable wet and unstable wet-dry conditions; unstable wet-dry conditions predominant after A.D. 900.			
Chenopodiaceae-Amaranthus / Compositae — Minor shifts	Scour-and-fill and quiet deposition; cienegas decrease in areal extent; slow and fast runoff. Shallow integrated channels cut; deposition continued in some cienegas; fast runoff.	Unstable wet-dry conditions; probably not as intense as those after A.D. 900.			900
					600
					300
	Maximum extent of cienegas as little fluvial material was deposited in area; slow runoff.			M_1 1860 B.P. Av. (Shell)	
				M_2 2310 B.P. Av. (Shell)	A.D. 1
Pinus, Quercus, and Cyperaceae	Influx of fluvial-laid sediments; no pronounced channeling; slow and fast runoff.	Stable to fairly stable wet conditions; little evidence of strong unstable wet-dry conditions.		Arizona EE:2:30 } 3660-1950 B.P. (Ariz.)	
				Arizona EE:2:35 } 2570 B.P.Av.(Ariz.) 2800 B.P. (Shell)	500 B.C.
	Cienega and lacustrine deposits; little fluvial material; slow runoff.				
				Unit 7 3570 B.P. (Shell)	1000
	—?— —?—	Probably transitional between unstable wet-dry and stable wet conditions.			
	—?— —?—				2000
	Downcutting; fast and sporadic runoff.	Unstable wet-dry conditions.	Altithermal		6000
			Anathermal		8000

The prehistoric Hohokam culture of the Tucson area was a product of distinctive influences converging from two directions: the Hohokam culture of the Gila River Basin of eastern Arizona and the Mogollon culture of eastern Arizona and western New Mexico. Diagnostic material culture traits in common with the Gila River Basin Hohokam are: (1) ceremonial architecture such as earth-constructed ball courts; (2) jacal house-in-a-pit dwellings; (3) cremation burial of the dead in pits; (4) ceramic forms and design styles that are regional variants of Gila River patterns; (5) carved, etched, and painted shell ornaments (Pomeroy 1959); (6) an emphasis on carved, pecked, and ground stone artifacts; (7) surplus irrigation farming of maize, beans, and cotton; and (8) widespread reciprocal trade in foodstuffs and craft items. The cultural features of the Tucson area that stem from the Mogollon culture (Wheat 1955) are: (1) use of deep pit houses with lateral ramp entries; (2) inhumation of the dead; and (3) the technique of polishing the surface of ceramic vessels after the application of the painted design.

The basic cultural patterns practiced by the prehistoric peoples of the Tucson area were Hohokam in orientation, but their geographic location, peripheral to this center of development, placed them under minor influences from the Mogollon culture. This peripheral characteristic is even more pronounced in the Empire Valley, which is southeast of Tucson nearer the area of influence of the Mogollon culture. Moving eastward, the progressive decrease of Hohokam material culture is reflected in the absence of certain traits in the Empire Valley: (1) ball courts were not reported from surveys (Swanson 1951); and (2) there was little use of shell ornaments or carved stone artifacts. This material impoverishment probably reflects less complexity in the religious, political, and economic aspects of the culture.

Taxonomic grouping of the Empire Valley culture with that of the Tucson area rather than with the Mogollon culture is based on ceramic affiliations that serve as a diagnostic index for the study of prehistoric cultural relationships and lines of development in the Southwest. The ceramic tradition of the Empire Valley is a regional variant of the Tucson styles referred to as the Santa Cruz Red-on-brown series (Colton 1955: 6).

3. GEOCHRONOLOGY AND DATING

Alluvial stratigraphic units were used as the basic framework to show the relative and superpositional placement of associated environmental and cultural data. Time correlations for the earlier events were accomplished through the radiocarbon method of age determination. Later events were dated by ceramic and historical information. Throughout the history of Cienega Valley there have been some environmental changes that reflect minor climatic fluctuations during the past 3000 years (see Fig. 2.16).

RADIOCARBON DATING

Radiocarbon dates reported herein were supplied in 1957 and 1958 by the Radiocarbon Age Determination Laboratory of the University of Arizona and the Exploration and Production Research Division of the Shell Oil Company, Houston, Texas (Table 3.1). The solid-carbon method developed by Willard F. Libby and his coworkers was used in processing samples at the University of Arizona Laboratory (Wise and Shutler 1958; Shutler and Damon 1959). The Shell laboratory used a gas method. Samples collected principally by Shutler and Eddy were run by the University of Arizona Laboratory, and the Shell Company processed the samples collected by Martin (Martin, Schoenwetter, and Arms 1961, table 6). Samples recounted using the carbon dioxide method and more recent calibrations are listed in Appendix C.

TABLE 3.1
Radiocarbon Dates for Cienega Valley
Samples analyzed in 1958, except A-74 (1957)
For dates analyzed after 1958 and Christian calendar calibrations (1982), see Appendix C

Provenience	Sample Number	University of Arizona Laboratory	Sample Number	Shell Development Laboratory
ARIZONA EE:2:30				
Unit 4				
Test 1, Pit 1	A-74	1950 ± 200 B.P.		
Test 3, Pit 11	A-85	2550 ± 330 B.P.		
Pit 14	A-86a	3080 ± 300 B.P.		
	A-86b	3660 ± 400 B.P.		
	A-86c	3180 ± 300 B.P.		
	A-86 av.	3300 ± 230 B.P.		
ARIZONA EE:2:35				
Unit 5				
Pit 3			Sh-5356	2800 ± 190 B.P.
Pit 4	A-87	2610 ± 250 B.P.		
	A-89a	3180 ± 300 B.P.		
	A-89b	2620 ± 200 B.P.		
	A-89c	2520 ± 300 B.P.		
	A-89 av.	2770 ± 170 B.P.		
Section MC-5				
Unit 3				
M₁ Marker Bed	A-88a	2980 ± 300 B.P.		
	A-88b	2740 ± 250 B.P.		
	A-88 av.	2860 ± 210 B.P.		
			Sh-5664a	1940 ± 170 B.P.
			Sh-5664b	1760 ± 190 B.P.
			Sh-5664 av.	1860 ± 130 B.P.
			Sh-5358	1850 ± 150 B.P.
M₂ Marker Bed			Sh-5665	2470 ± 200 B.P.
			Sh-5389	2150 ± 140 B.P.
Section MC-4*				
Unit 7			Sh-5357	3570 ± 210 B.P.

*Gelogical section (see Fig. 1.3).
Sample A-74: Wise and Shutler 1958: 74.
Samples A-85–89: Shutler and Damon 1959: 60–61.
Shell Laboratory dates: Martin, Schoenwetter, and Arms 1961, table 6.

Sufficient quantities of charcoal for radiocarbon age determination tests were obtained from cooking pits of the San Pedro stage at Arizona EE:2:30 and EE:2:35. Charcoal concentrations occurred in the lower third of the cooking pits in association with hearthstones and damp, sandy to clayey fill. The charcoal was removed in chunks, some of which were large enough for species identification (see Table 2.1). After collecting the samples with a penknife, the carbon was stored in a polyethylene bag as a precaution against contamination. Several samples were taken from two peaty deposits—M_1 and M_2 marker beds near Section MC–5 (Martin, Schoenwetter, and Arms 1961, table 6). Insofar as possible, rootlets were avoided and a minimum of nonorganic matter was included in the samples.

Radiocarbon dates from the cooking pits at Arizona EE:2:30 indicate a range of more than 1300 years, extending from about 1300 B.C. to A.D. 1. The youngest date approximating the end of the midden occupation is 1950 ± 200 B.P. (A–74), obtained from Cooking Pit 1 (for years before the present, A.D. 1950 is the base date). The early span of habitation is indicated by a 2550 ± 330 B.P. (A–85) date from Pit 11 and the still older average date of 3300 ± 230 B.P. (A–86 av.) obtained from three runs on a carbon sample from Pit 14. It is unusual to find such an extended period of time involved in a single site. This may be accounted for by the specialized environmental and, perhaps, by economic features occurring at this locality, as well as by indeterminate factors within the dating method. The dating of Arizona EE:2:30 appears to span nearly the entire age range of the San Pedro stage, from about 1000 B.C. to the beginning of the Christian era.

Radiocarbon dates on charcoal from Cooking Pits 3 and 4 at Arizona EE:2:35 were analyzed by both the University of Arizona (2 samples) and Shell laboratories (1 sample). These dates, which are in general agreement, range from 2610 ± 250 B.P. (A–87) to 2800 ± 190 B.P. (Sh–5356) and correspond in time with the occupation at Arizona EE:2:30. The agreement of the dates at this locality serves as a check on the sampling procedures and methods used by the two laboratories and on the postulated cultural equivalence of the two preceramic sites.

In addition to dates on cultural material, a number of natural deposits produced organic samples suitable for radiocarbon analysis. A sample taken from Unit 7 near Section MC–4 and Arizona EE:2:12 gave a date of 3570 ± 210 B.P. (Sh–5357; Martin, Schoenwetter, and Arms 1961, table 6). This date is the oldest we obtained in the study area and indicates the magnitude of time involved in the late Recent alluvial deposition. Radiocarbon dates from five samples collected from the M_1 and M_2 marker beds at Section MC–5 range in age from 1860 ± 130 B.P. (Sh–5664 av.) to 2860 ± 210 B.P. (A–88 av.), which approximates the range of dates obtained upstream from Arizona EE:2:30. However, analysis of these dates reveals a discrepancy. The University of Arizona date (A–88 av.) for the M_1 marker bed is exactly 1000 years earlier than the date obtained by Shell (Sh–5664 av.). The analysis of the other four samples, two from each marker bed, reveals that samples from the same bed have closely corresponding dates and the two sets of dates agree with the time sequence of the alluvial stratigraphy. Thus, dates from the M_2 marker bed range from 2150 ± 140 B.P. (Sh–5389) to 2470 ± 200 B.P. (Sh–5665) and are significantly older than the dates of 1860 ± 130 B.P. (Sh–5664 av.) and 1850 ± 150 (Sh–5358) obtained from the M_1 marker bed. The date run by the University of Arizona Laboratory (Sample A–88 av.) for this location is inconsistent with the results provided by Shell. [More recent dating by the University of Arizona resolves this discrepancy; see Appendix C.]

The Shell laboratory dates from the M_2 marker bed correlate this marsh deposit with the San Pedro occupation at Arizona EE:2:30. This correlation is also indicated by the alluvial stratigraphy, and it suggests an association that may have provided an incentive for human inhabitants to frequent this preceramic station.

CERAMIC DATING

Intrusive northern pottery found at the Snaketown site in the Gila River Basin (Gladwin and others 1937, fig. 106) provides an extension of the tree-ring dated ceramic chronology of the Colorado Plateau into southern Arizona. The ceramics of southeastern Arizona can be correlated with the Gila River Hohokam pottery types through trade wares.

Sampling of sites by surface collection was done selectively. We felt that more information could be obtained by securing diagnostic painted ceramics than by collecting a proportionately representative sample of all types. Because of this, the proportion of painted sherds to plain wares is heavily weighted. For this reason, the number of sherds is not reported, but rather emphasis is placed on the occurrence of types in the ceramic complex (see Table 2.4).

The cultural chronology at the Snaketown site was established mainly in 200-year periods ranging from 300 B.C. to A.D. 1400. The occupation is best dated between A.D. 500 and 1400 (Gladwin and others 1937, fig. 106). The preceding 800 years are mostly estimated. The major anchor point of the chronology, based on the quantity and reliability of intrusive trade sherds, is the Sacaton phase of the Sedentary period that has an age range of A.D. 900 to 1100.

Subsequent to the original work at the Snaketown site, the lower limit of this cultural chronology was modified. This change is based on radiocarbon dates from preceramic sites in southeastern Arizona and west-central New Mexico. The dates from both areas indicate that the preceramic period was later in this area than the original estimate of 500 B.C. reported by Sayles and Antevs (1941, fig. 19). Two dates in southeastern Arizona were obtained from samples collected by Sayles at sites of the San Pedro stage. At Arizona BB:6 an average date of 2090 ± 250 B.P. (A–71) was derived from a prepottery level exposed in Peppersauce Wash, southeast of Oracle (Shutler and Damon 1959: 60), and a younger date of 1762 ± 430 B.P. (Johnson 1951: 15, Sample No. 518) was derived from charcoal at the type site of the San Pedro stage, Benson:5:10 (Gila Pueblo). Investigation at Tularosa Cave (Martin 1963) in west-central New Mexico produced an early radiocarbon averaging date of 2145 ± 160 (Johnson 1951: 17) for the Pine Lawn phase of the Mogollon culture. This phase was accepted as the earliest pottery-producing horizon in the Southwest (Haury 1957: 22).

To reiterate, radiocarbon dates on late preceramic sites in southern Arizona are not later than A.D. 200. One date from an early ceramic level in west-central New Mexico is 200 B.C. If there is a certain degree of latitude in the radiocarbon dating technique, then A.D. 1 can be arbitrarily taken as the time for the appearance of pottery in southern Arizona and western New Mexico outside of the main drainage of the Gila River Basin. These findings are comparable to those of Haury (1950, fig. 117) for Ventana Cave in southwestern Arizona. [For more recent dating, see Appendix C.]

Data in Cienega Valley supporting A.D. 1 as the time for the appearance of pottery consist of two lines of reasoning: (1) a date of 1950 ± 200 B.P. from the preceramic San Pedro site, Arizona EE:2:30, and (2) the close similarity in the stratigraphic position of this site and an early Pioneer period component at Arizona EE:2:10. Both sites rest on a former valley surface cut on Unit 100, and both are overlain by Unit 3 deposits that contain a nearly unbroken sequence of later Hohokam ceramic components. Thus, it is possible that only a short period of time may have separated the occupations of these San Pedro and early Pioneer period sites.

The updating of the early ceramic phases outside of the main drainage of the Gila River Basin necessitates a compression of the Pioneer period from the original estimated beginning date of 300 B.C. (Gladwin and others 1937) to A.D. 1. In 1958 Emil Haury estimated the length of Pioneer period phases as follows: Vahki and Estrella, 300 years; Sweetwater, 100 years; and Snaketown, 200 years. These estimates terminate the period at A.D. 600. This view shortens the Cañada del Oro phase (Gila Butte phase in the Snaketown sequence) by 100 years from the original span of A.D. 500 to 700 given in the Snaketown report (Gladwin and others 1937). The Rillito phase (Santa Cruz) remains unchanged but the dates for the Rincon phase (Sacaton) have been extended 100 years, from A.D. 900 to 1200. This time change is due to the late occurrence of Sacaton Red-on-buff in the eastern part of its distribution in southeastern Arizona.

Classic period subunits are dated from A.D. 1200 to 1300 for the Tanque Verde phase and A.D. 1300 to 1400 for the Tucson phase (Hayden 1957: 122). There is no indication of occupation in Cienega Valley between A.D. 1500 and the later part of the nineteenth century, the beginning of historical occupation.

HISTORICAL DATING

Perusal of the files in the Arizona Pioneers Historical Society resulted in the establishment of an approximate date for early ranching operations by the Sanford family in Cienega Valley. According to these records, the Sanfords moved into the Empire Valley area in the early 1870s and in 1876 the Sanford property was bought by Walter Vail, who founded the Empire Ranch. In all probability, the main ranch building, the corral adjacent to Arizona EE:2:14, and the buried rock floor (Arizona EE:2:38) were used during this time.

AGE OF THE ALLUVIAL UNITS

The oldest alluvial unit in Cienega Valley, Unit 100, was laid down on Cretaceous rocks, and it may include several deposits of late Cenozoic age. Two or more levels of terraces, probably of late Pleistocene age, were formed on the deposits of Unit 100. The age of Unit 100 may extend from late Pleistocene back to the Pliocene.

The erosion that formed the terraces adjoining Cienega Valley and the erosion surface beneath the late Recent alluvium (Units 1–7; see Fig. 2.16) began during the late part of the Pleistocene and was terminated by the late Recent alluviation. Any alluvial deposition that occurred during early Recent time may have been scoured out as soon as it was deposited or it may lie buried away from the present erosional channels. The residual-soil zone developed on Unit 100 and underlying Unit 3 at Arizona EE:2:10 was probably formed during the latest Pleistocene and early Recent times.

Alluvial Units 1 through 7 were deposited in late Recent time, or since approximately 2000 B.C. (see Figs. 1.6, 2.16). The exposures show intertonguing and gradational contacts between Units 3 through 6, indicating that sedimentation was continuous throughout the time of deposition of these units in parts of Cienega Valley. The only major stratigraphic breaks in the area occur between Unit 3 and the Sanford formation (Unit 2) and the present period of arroyo cutting at the end of the deposition of Unit 1. The late Recent age is primarily supported by the dating of cultural remains buried in the deposits. Artifacts of the San Pedro stage are buried in Units 4 and 5 and material of the Hohokam culture is embedded in Unit 3. Further support is supplied by the radiocarbon dates taken from Units 3, 4, 5, and 7, which range from approximately 1500 B.C. to A.D. 200.

Unit 7 has a maximum age range of 2000 B.C. to A.D. 1200 or 1300. A radiocarbon date of approximately 1500 B.C. comes from this unit near Arizona EE:2:12. At this location Unit 7 intertongues with Units 5 and 6. The age range of Unit 7 is long in comparison with the other alluvial units, and as noted in Chapter 1, it represents an accumulation of residual mantle along the sides of the valley. It is therefore not suitable for correlation, specific dating, and the determination of environmental relationships.

The age of Unit 6 can be inferred only from the more specific dating of Unit 5, which, in the places where it has been dated, has an age of about 1500 B.C. to 800 B.C. Because Unit 6 intertongues and correlates with at least part of Unit 5, its deposition probably began before 1500 B.C. and may have terminated about 500 B.C.

The time of deposition for Unit 5 is about the same as that for Unit 6. Three radiocarbon dates taken from the cultural remains in Unit 5 at Arizona EE:2:35 fall within a span of only 125 years, from 825 to 700 B.C. This age is supported by the remains of San Pedro stage material interbedded in the unit. The radiocarbon date of approximately 1500 B.C. obtained from Unit 7 near Arizona EE:2:12 indicates that Unit 5 in this area of Cienega Valley is older than the Unit 5 deposits near Arizona EE:2:36, and that deposition may have started before 1500 B.C. Thus, the age range of all Unit 5 deposits may extend from before 1500 B.C. to slightly later than 500 B.C.

Stratigraphic studies indicate that Unit 4 is equivalent to the upper part of Unit 6, Unit 5, and almost all of Unit 3. Unit 4 deposits were laid down in ponds and swamps—the cienega deposits of the area. Both Units 3 and 5 are composed of sand and gravel brought in by streams that flowed into the swampy areas. Only one archaeological site, Arizona EE:2:12 of the San Pedro stage, has been reported from Unit 4, although occupation of the extensive site at Arizona EE:2:30 apparently was concurrent with the deposition of Unit 4. This correlation is based on the stratigraphic relationships of the M_1 and M_2 marker beds and the eastward extensions of Unit 4 cienega deposits at Section MC-5 with Arizona EE:2:30, and on the radiocarbon dates obtained from the site and the marker beds. These dates range from 1000 B.C. to A.D. 200, but they are from the lower part of the unit; therefore, including the remainder of the unit that is a lateral equivalent of Unit 3, Unit 4 has a maximum age range of approximately 1000 B.C. to slightly more than A.D. 900.

While the upper part of Unit 4 was being deposited in the swampy areas, the silty sand of Unit 3 was being laid down in the eastern part of Cienega Valley. At Arizona EE:2:30, Unit 3 was deposited on top of the San Pedro stage midden and pits, although no material from this stage was observed in the unit. Archaeological sites assigned to the Hohokam culture, ranging from Vahki-Estrella to possibly the Tanque Verde phase, are preserved in Unit 3. Dating by these cultural phases, and by the radiocarbon age determinations of the M_1 and M_2 marker beds, gives an age range of about A.D. 1 to A.D. 1200 or 1300 for the deposition of Unit 3 (see Table 3.1). The onset of Unit 3 deposition began at different times in various parts of Cienega Valley. The oldest deposit of the unit is at Section MC-5, where deposition began shortly before the time of Christ. The shortest span of Unit 3 deposition is in the area of the upper and lower falls of Cienega Creek near Arizona EE:2:35, where the age ranges from about A.D. 900 to 1200 or 1300. Figure 3.1 summarizes the dating of Unit 3 in selected parts of Cienega Valley.

The Sanford formation (Unit 2), underlying Unit 1, fills deep channels and arroyos cut into Unit 3 and older units. The formation is dissected by present arroyos. Historical occupation seems to have been concurrent with the later part of the Sanford formation deposition at Arizona EE:2:38. Tanque Verde phase remains were found in the unit at Arizona EE:2:41 and elsewhere. It is difficult to determine whether the Tanque Verde remains were on the surface cut on Unit 3, in the topmost layers of Unit 3, or in the Sanford formation. Possibly, Tanque Verde material is present at two or all three of these horizons. The exact stratigraphic position is masked by the formation of the soil, developed in part on Unit 3, that comprises most of the Sanford formation. The age of the arroyo cutting period that preceded

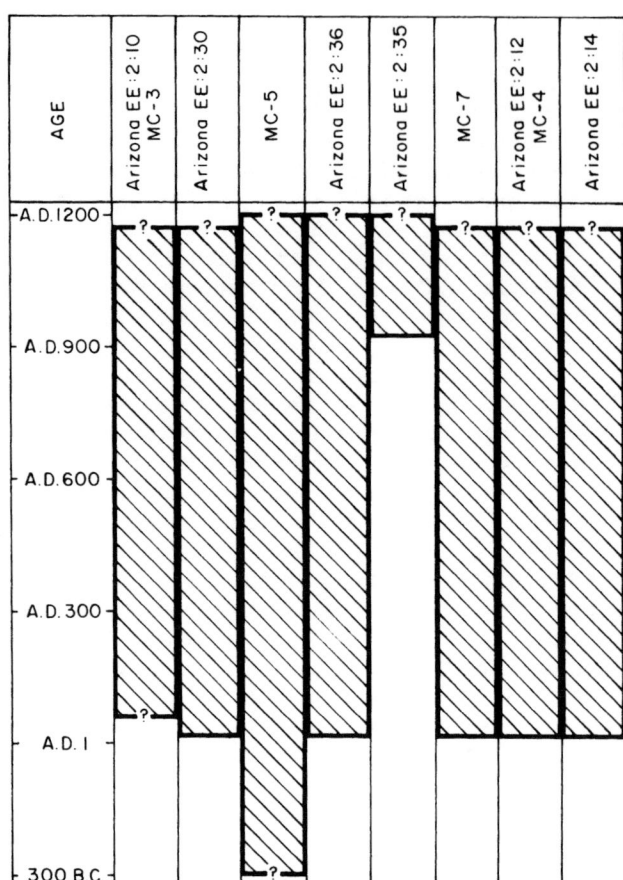

Figure 3.1. Age range of Unit 3 sediments in Cienega Valley.

deposition of the formation cannot be determined exactly because of the limited distribution of the arroyos formed at that time. In one of the fossil arroyos near Arizona EE:2:10 the cutting must be younger than A.D. 900, because the arroyo is carved into Unit 3 deposits containing Rincon phase and older material. Because Rincon and Tanque Verde phase materials are associated with the uppermost beds of Unit 3 or the surface formed at the same time as the arroyo cutting, the erosion and arroyo cutting probably occurred after A.D. 1000 or 1100. If the cutting of the arroyos and the deposition of the Sanford formation (indicating strong changes in the environmental conditions) had an influence on the marked decline in occupation between the Tanque Verde and Tucson phases, then the arroyo cutting may have occurred during the A.D. 1200s and the deposition of the Sanford formation may have started at approximately A.D. 1300. In summary, the Sanford formation, based on the available archaeological evidence, has a maximum age range extending from about A.D. 1200 to 1875. In Cienega Valley it is more likely that deposition began shortly after A.D. 1200.

The erosion preceding the deposition of Unit 1 terminated deposition of the Sanford formation. Unit 1 was deposited slightly before and during the early part of the present period of arroyo cutting. Its age range, therefore, is short—from A.D. 1875 to 1900. According to local ranchers, this is the time when arroyos were being formed in the Empire Valley.

TABLE 3.2
Rates of Deposition of the Recent Alluvium in Cienega Valley

Location	Approximate thickness (meters)	Approximate deposition time in years	Average rate of deposition (cmpy)	Stratigraphic interval
Unit 1				
Section MC–1	1.7	25	6.71	
MC–2	0.9	25	3.66	
MC–4	0.3–1.5	25	1.21–6.10	
MC–5	0.8	25	3.10	
MC–7	0.5	25	1.83[a]	
Unit 2, Sanford Formation				
Section MC–1	1.2	550	0.21	
MC–2	4.9	550	0.91[b]	
MC–3	1.1	550	0.18	
MC–4	0.3–1.5	550	0.06–0.31	
MC–5	0.8	550	0.15	
MC–6	0.6	550	0.06	
Unit 3				
Section MC–1	1.5	900?[c]	0.15[c]	
MC–3	0.3	900	0.34[c]	
MC–4	3.3	900–1200	0.37–0.27[c]	
Unit 3a				
Section MC–3	0.9	300	0.31[c]	
MC–5	1.4	300	0.46[c]	
MC–6	0.9–1.8	300	0.31–0.61	
Total Recent Alluvium				
Section MC–1	4.1	1700	0.24	Units 1–3
MC–3	5.2	1700	0.31	Units 1–3
MC–4	7.0	3500	0.21	Units 1–7
MC–5	5.2	2300	0.21	Units 1–3
Arizona EE:2:35	5.6	2800	0.18	Units 1–5
100 feet downstream of lower falls	12.1	4000[d]	0.31	Units 1–7
Cienega Creek pollen profile	6.7	2800[d]	0.24	Units 1–5

a. May be more than 25 years.
b. Includes the filled channel.
c. Upper part stripped by post-Unit 3–pre-unit 2 erosion.
d. Age estimated.

RATES OF ALLUVIATION

Before attempting to establish an idea of the rate of the late Recent alluvial deposition in Cienega Valley, seven major difficulties should be emphasized: (1) the contacts between the several alluvial units and the beds within the units, for the most part, have been arbitrarily chosen (the contact between some of the thinner beds may make up as much as 25 percent of the total thickness of the adjoining beds); (2) the alluvial deposits are thicker in the center of the valley than they are along the sides, where deposition did not occur until later because of the overlapping of alluvial sediments on the older rocks; (3) variations in thickness can be caused by differential compaction of the sediments; (4) knowledge of the periods of deposition of all the alluvial units is incomplete; (5) the dating of the alluvial units and beds within the units is based on both archaeological sites and radiocarbon dates, which are only approximations in the time sequence; (6) the stratigraphic relationships of the alluvial units, especially the intertonguing of deposits laid down in different sedimentary environments, affect the overall and specific rates of deposition in different areas of Cienega Valley; and (7) some of the units are separated by erosional contacts indicating a break in deposition and some missing time, and some have soils on them indicating periods of nondeposition.

Three types of alluvial deposition are represented in Cienega Valley: sediments laid down in fluvial or cienega environments and deposition of residual-soil zones. The fluvial deposits, chiefly Units 1, 3, and 5, present the poorest record for determining a rate of deposition because the channeling and scour-fill types of sedimentation cause innumerable minor breaks in deposition. In a fluvial environment, the deposits may represent only a small percentage of the total time assigned to that particular unit. The cienega deposits of Units 2, 4, and 6 are characterized by fairly stable depositional conditions. Cienega deposition is considered to be more or less continuous with no erosional breaks. However, relatively short intervals of nondeposition probably interrupt sedimentation from time to time. The residual-soil deposits form the most stable and continuous depositional types of the area. The formation of a residual-soil mantle occurs in areas where no erosion or rapid alluviation takes place.

The rates listed in Table 3.2 represent only the general magnitude of possible rates of alluvial deposition. These rates should be considered only as having approximate value. The figures appear to indicate certain general consistencies in rates of deposition for similar types of deposits. Generally, Unit 1 had the fastest rate of deposition—as much as 6.1 cmpy (cm per year) at Sections MC–1 and MC–4. Near the confluence of Matty Wash and Cienega Creek, however, the rate was less than 1.52 cmpy. Study of the Unit 1 sediments in both areas helped to confirm the differences in the rates. The investigation showed that coarser deposits were laid down along Matty Wash nearer the source of the material than along Cienega Creek. The Sanford formation has the lowest rate of deposition (0.12 cmpy) in the area where it occurs as a residual-soil mantle. In the areas on the margins of the floodplain where some fluvial sediments have been deposited, it has rates of more than 0.21 cmpy.

The rates of deposition for Units 3 and 4, although deposited in different sedimentary environments, range between 0.15 cmpy and 0.61 cmpy. These units have an average rate of 0.31 cmpy. Unit 4 sediments represent nearly continuous deposition, but because parts of the Unit 3 sediments were laid down in channels, many breaks occur in the alluvial record.

Information on the depositional rates of Units 5 and 6 is insufficient, although they probably have a rate of less than 0.15 cmpy—a conclusion supported by the lithology and bedding features.

The average rate of deposition in Cienega Valley for the total late Recent alluvial sequence, in areas on the floodplain that are free from effects of the valley sides, ranges between 0.21 cmpy and 0.31 cmpy. The mean rate of deposition in the valley is approximately 0.24 cmpy. It seems likely that had no erosion or breaks in the deposition occurred, the total thickness of the alluvium would be several times the present preserved thickness, and the rates of deposition would be considerably greater than the ones listed in Table 3.2. This hypothesis is supported principally by the amount and distribution of the channeling that can be observed in the alluvial sequence.

4. PAST ENVIRONMENTS

The study of past environmental changes is based on hydrogeological, biological, and cultural evidence. The alluvial stratigraphy, which provides the general framework or time-stratigraphic sequence, has been dated by cultural remains and radiocarbon age determinations (see Fig. 2.16). All evidence must be viewed in relationship to the alluvial stratigraphy in order to interpret changes in the environment and to reconstruct the environmental history.

Each alluvial unit represents a deposit that was laid down in a general type of depositional environment. Each unit displays particular lithological characteristics and types of sedimentary features. Deposits with similar features are grouped together for purposes of mapping and tracing. The principal sedimentary features that aid in interpretations of environment are general lithology, inclusion of carbonaceous material, type of bedding, amount of channeling, and presence of soil zones. In order to make environmental interpretations, the distribution and lateral changes in the lithology and sedimentary features of each unit, the beds within the units, and the intertonguing between the units must be examined in detail. The distribution of cienega deposits, fluvial deposits, and channels or arroyos is shown in Figure 4.1.

LATE RECENT ENVIRONMENTAL FLUCTUATIONS

The erosion of early Recent and late Pleistocene time, which lowered the valley floor by 15 m to 30 m, was brought to a close approximately 2000 B.C. by the beginning of the late Recent alluviation in Cienega Valley. This period of erosion is correlated with the Anathermal and Altithermal periods defined by Antevs (1955). Intertonguing of Units 3, 4, 5, and 6 indicates that deposition was essentially continuous until A.D. 1100 or 1200. During this time, Matty Wash and other tributary streams of Cienega Creek deposited relatively fine-grained material, regardless of shifts in environmental influences. As a result, the generally fine deposits forming the cienega beds of Units 4 and 6 are restricted to the central part of Cienega Valley and to areas away from the main tributary streams, whereas the coarse fluvial deposits are found mainly along the margins of the valley and the tributaries (Fig. 4.1).

The deposits comprising Units 4, 5, and 6 contain more clay and silt, the individual beds extend farther laterally, and the bedding is more uniform than in Unit 3. Throughout the area, Unit 3 is sandier, contains more gravel, and displays more cross-bedding features, lenticular bedding, and channels than Units 4, 5, and 6. Interpretation of the lithologic types and sedimentary features indicates that Units 4 and 6 were laid down in swamps and a few ponds, and that Units 3 and 5 were deposited by streams. Analysis of all the sedimentary features reveals that throughout the deposition of Units 3 through 6, or roughly from 1500 B.C. to A.D. 1100 or 1200, stream flow was relatively sluggish and the deposition relatively stable. Because these alluvial units were laid down in fluvial and cienega types of depositional environments—environments mainly controlled by climatic influences (chiefly precipitation)—the climate may have been generally stable and fairly moist (see Fig. 2.16). Channeling in Units 3 and 4 indicates that some change in environmental conditions took place from time to time. The environment gradually became drier and less stable after some peak, perhaps between 1500 and 1000 B.C., until the increasing aridity resulted in the final drying up and decreased areal extent of the cienegas between A.D. 900 and 1200.

Erosion and arroyo trenching, later filled by Unit 2 sediments (Sanford formation), terminated the deposition of Unit 3. The change from deposition to erosion seems to have been gradual, considering the scour-and-fill depositional features displayed in the upper part of Unit 3—principally channeling, lenticular bedding, and gravel lenses. These features indicate sporadic runoff, flash floods, and, in general, somewhat unstable environmental conditions. Such features are not commonly found in the lower part of Unit 3. The arroyo cutting may have occurred during the A.D. 1200s or slightly earlier, most likely between A.D. 1100 and 1300. The dating of this erosion is based on the Rincon phase material (A.D. 900–1200) buried in the upper part of Unit 3 and on scattered sherds of the Tanque Verde phase (A.D. 1200–1300) found in the Sanford formation. The erosion must have been caused largely by an environmental shift after A.D. 900 from stable to less stable conditions or wetter to drier conditions. This environmental shift resulted in the drying up of the Unit 4 cienegas, the scour-and-fill deposition of Unit 3, and the termination of Unit 3 deposition when conditions favored erosion and arroyo cutting.

The Sanford formation is characterized by thin-bedded sediments laid down in the previously formed channels, and by a residual soil zone and swampy deposits that form a mantle over much of the area. The depositional features such as organic material present in the thinly bedded sediments and other deposits that make up the formation, and the absence of gravel, strongly suggest that deposition took

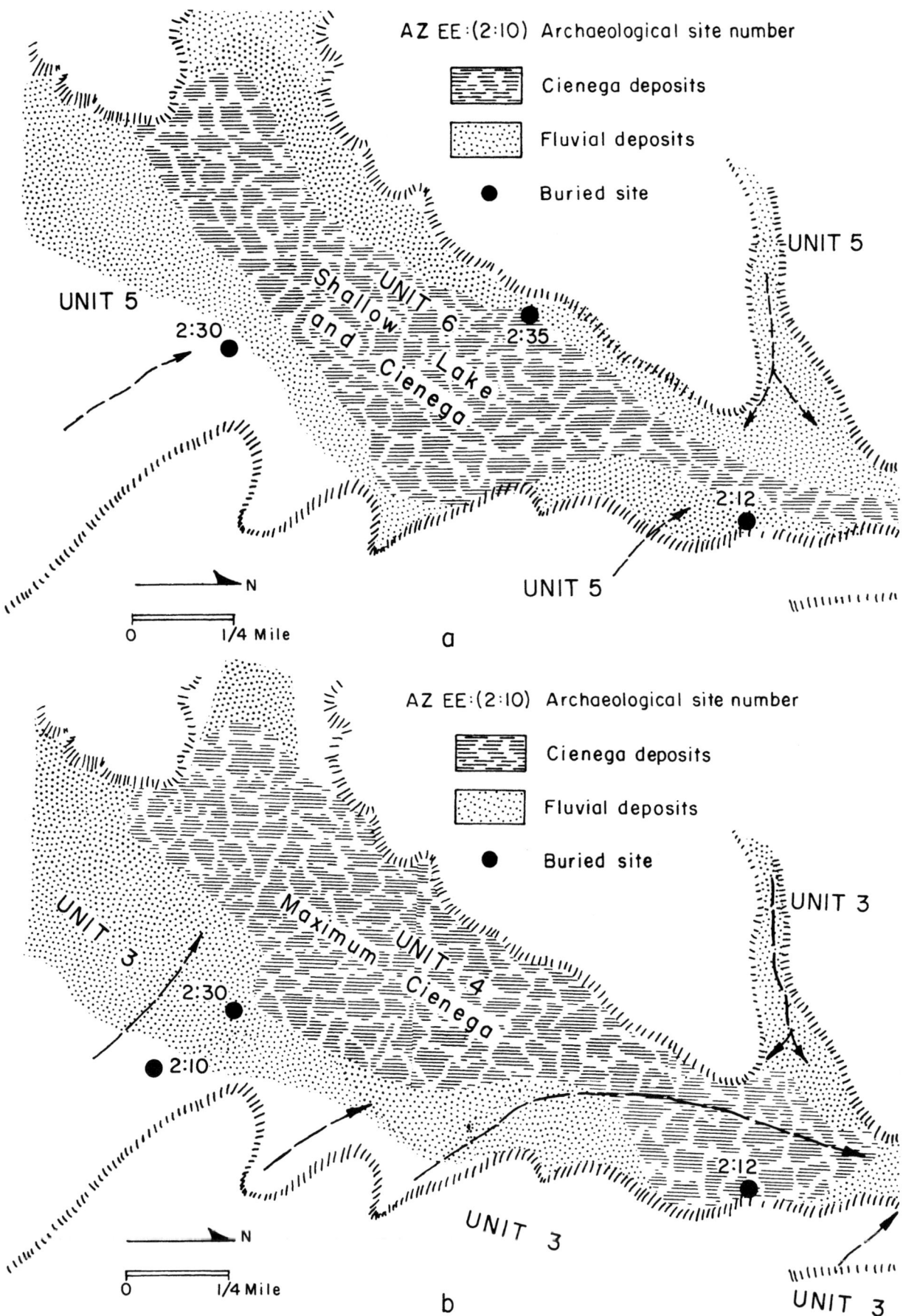

Figure 4.1. Late Recent environmental conditions and distribution of sites in Cienega Valley: *a*, alluvial environment during the deposition of Units 5 and 6 in early San Pedro times (1000 to 500 B.C.); *b*, alluvial environment during the deposition of the M_1 and M_2 marker beds in late San Pedro-early Pioneer times

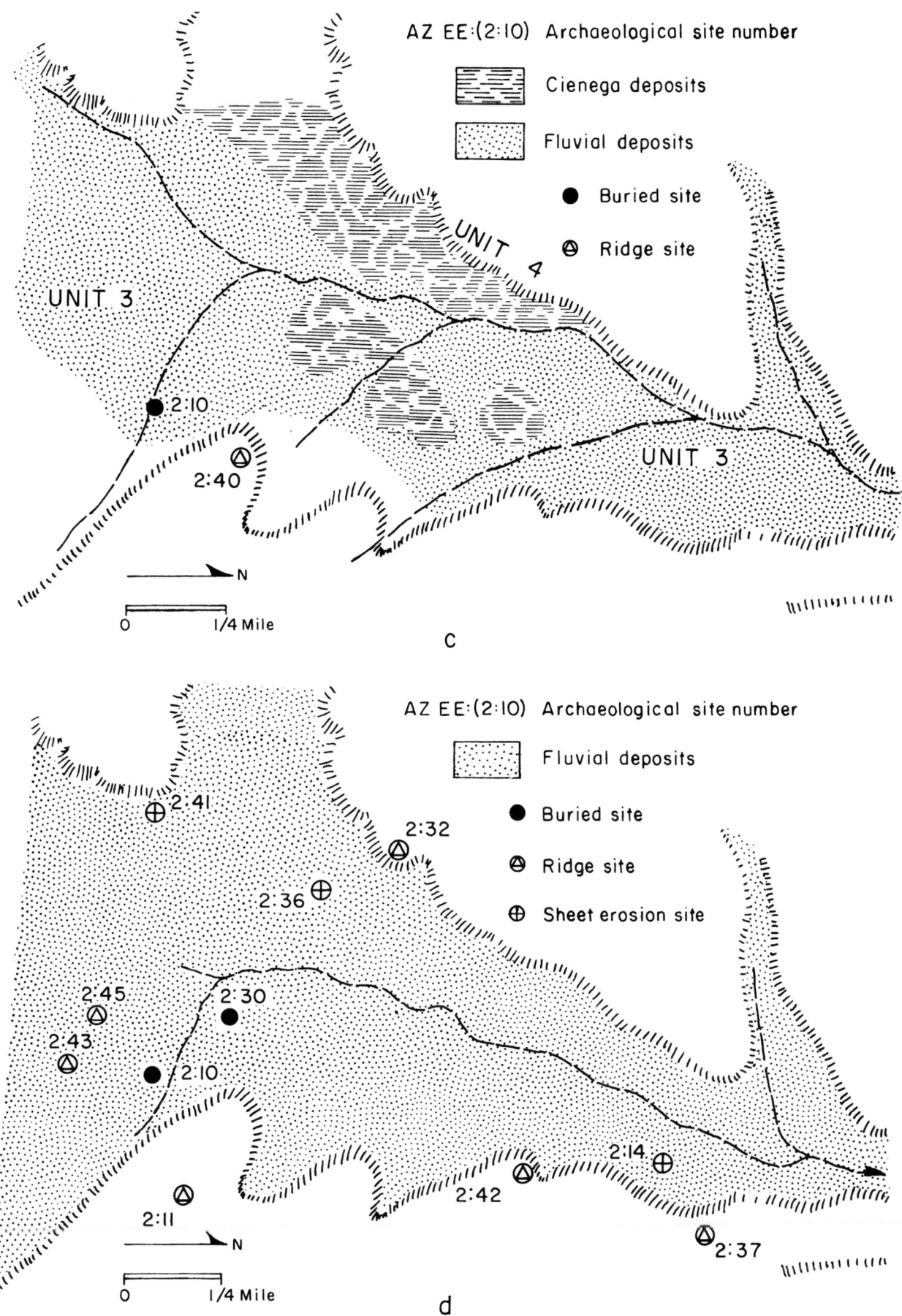

(about A.D. 1); *c*, development of drainage of Units 3 and 4 in late Pioneer times during the period of channeling (A.D. 200 to 600); *d*, distribution of the arroyos formed in late Sedentary or early Classic times (A.D. 1100 to 1300). Directions of drainage flows are indicated by arrows.

place in sluggish streams that were not subjected to much flash flooding, and that a relatively wet, stable depositional environment and climate prevailed (see Fig. 2.16). These environmental conditions contrast with those of both the period A.D. 900 to 1300 and the present. Within the area investigated there is no sedimentary break in the Sanford formation, but a half mile (0.8 km) north along Cienega Creek, the surface below a younger channel fill truncates the fill of an older channel. Both fills should be included as parts of the Sanford formation because not only are they lithologically similar to the formation in the area investigated, but also they underlie Unit 1 and overlie Unit 3. The presence of the younger channel indicates that at least once during the deposition of the Sanford formation conditions were such that deposition terminated and erosion was favored.

The cutting of shallow channels, which were filled by the sandy and gravelly sediments of Unit 1 and the scour-and-fill process, ended the deposition of the Sanford formation and began the initial phase of the present period of arroyo cutting. Rapid runoff and flash flooding are indicated by channeling and gravel deposition. Precipitation records compiled by the U.S. Weather Bureau show that precipitation was sporadic, and that the period from 1892 to 1904 was abnormally dry (Fig. 4.2). These conditions favor scour-and-fill deposition and erosion. Because arroyos were not conspicuous features in this reach of Cienega Creek until 1900, the intense dry period prior to 1905 may have aided the arroyo cutting. The cutting must also have been helped by the influx of flood runoff resulting from the high precipitation recorded in 1905 and in a few years following.

A comparison between the modern arroyos and those filled by the Sanford formation indicates that the depth and width of the present arroyos are much greater. Depths reached during both times of arroyo dissection are nearly the same at Arizona EE:2:10, but near the confluence of Matty Wash and Cienega Creek the present arroyos are nearly a meter deeper. A greater dissimilarity may be found in the amount of lateral cutting. In some places, the modern arroyo banks are more than 182 m apart, while those formed earlier are less than 31 m apart. The arroyos filled by the Sanford formation are located along Matty Wash and only in the northern part of the area (Fig. 4.1d) along Cienega Creek. The present arroyos extend across the entire area along Matty Wash and Cienega Creek, and upstream along many of their tributaries.

DRAINAGE PATTERN AND ENVIRONMENT OF UNITS 3 AND 4

Information on the distribution and development of ancient drainages was obtained from the study of Units 3 and 4. In the western part of Cienega Valley, a series of related stream channels and lenticular gravel beds can be traced from Unit 4 into Unit 3 without an apparent break in sedimentation. These channels were present at the same time that the finer-grained deposits were being laid down in adjoining areas. The erosion surface at the base of these channels was restricted only to the area of the channel. The erosion surface faded out laterally and could not be recognized in the sedimentary sequence a meter away. This type of channel is found between the lower falls of Cienega Creek and Section MC-7. There, a series of channels extends from the upper part of Unit 4 into the lower part of Unit 3, representing a time span of about 500 B.C. to A.D. 600. The lateral movement of the channels was approximately 91 m, with some 5 m of alluvium deposited. Another similar series of small channels exposed in Unit 3 near Arizona EE:2:30 shows a lateral shift of 91 m with a deposition of 2.4 m of alluvium. This series of channels ranges in age from about 50 B.C. to nearly A.D. 900. All these channels indicate that through-flowing streams were not only present in parts of Cienega Valley during the time of widespread cienega development, but were concurrent with the alluviation of the upper part of Unit 4 and the lower part of Unit 3.

Other buried channels containing some gravel and having relatively well-defined sides are present both upstream from Arizona EE:2:10 along Matty Wash, near Arizona EE:2:36, and at the lower falls along Cienega Creek. These channels, based on their stratigraphic position with relation to the archaeological sites, were cut sometime between A.D. 1 and 600, or possibly between A.D. 200 to 300 and 600. Considering the distribution of gravel beds in the deposits overlying these channels, the streams that cut the channels maintained courses until approximately A.D. 900.

After about A.D. 900, the network of channels cannot be recognized in the upper part of Unit 3. Even though many small channels are present in the upper part of Unit 3, the drainage appears to lack definition compared with the earlier drainage system that was present in Unit 4 and the lower part of Unit 3.

Interpretation of the channels (description, distribution, size, and association with the enclosing deposits) with respect to drainage patterns and implied environmental conditions indicates four relationships. (1) Although there is evidence of a few small, well-defined channels formed in B.C. times, those channels probably should not be interpreted as indicating a specific period or periods of erosion and channel formation. (2) The only period of channeling before the termination of Unit 3 deposition that seems to be associated with a shift in environmental conditions occurred sometime during A.D. 200 to 300 and 600, when the drainages were entrenched in an integrated set of channels throughout Cienega Valley (Fig. 4.1c). These channels may correlate with those formed near Douglas and described by Antevs (1955: 330) as having been cut during the Whitewater drought. (3) In general, alluviation (including the distribution of the cienegas) and the drainage patterns were relatively stable from about 50 B.C. to about A.D. 900. (4) The drainages established before A.D. 900 did not continue as recognizable units through the A.D. 900 to 1200 period, suggesting a change in environmental conditions around A.D. 900.

The deposits of Units 3 and 4 reflect some minor fluctuations in environmental conditions. The environment seems to have been stable with few apparent fluctuations until A.D. 200 to 300. That stability is reflected in the large amount of cienega-type deposition compared with the relatively small amount of sandy material brought in by the streams. The fine-grained fluvial deposits were laid down by slow-moving water. The channel cutting of about A.D. 200 or 300 to 600 suggests some unstable environmental conditions

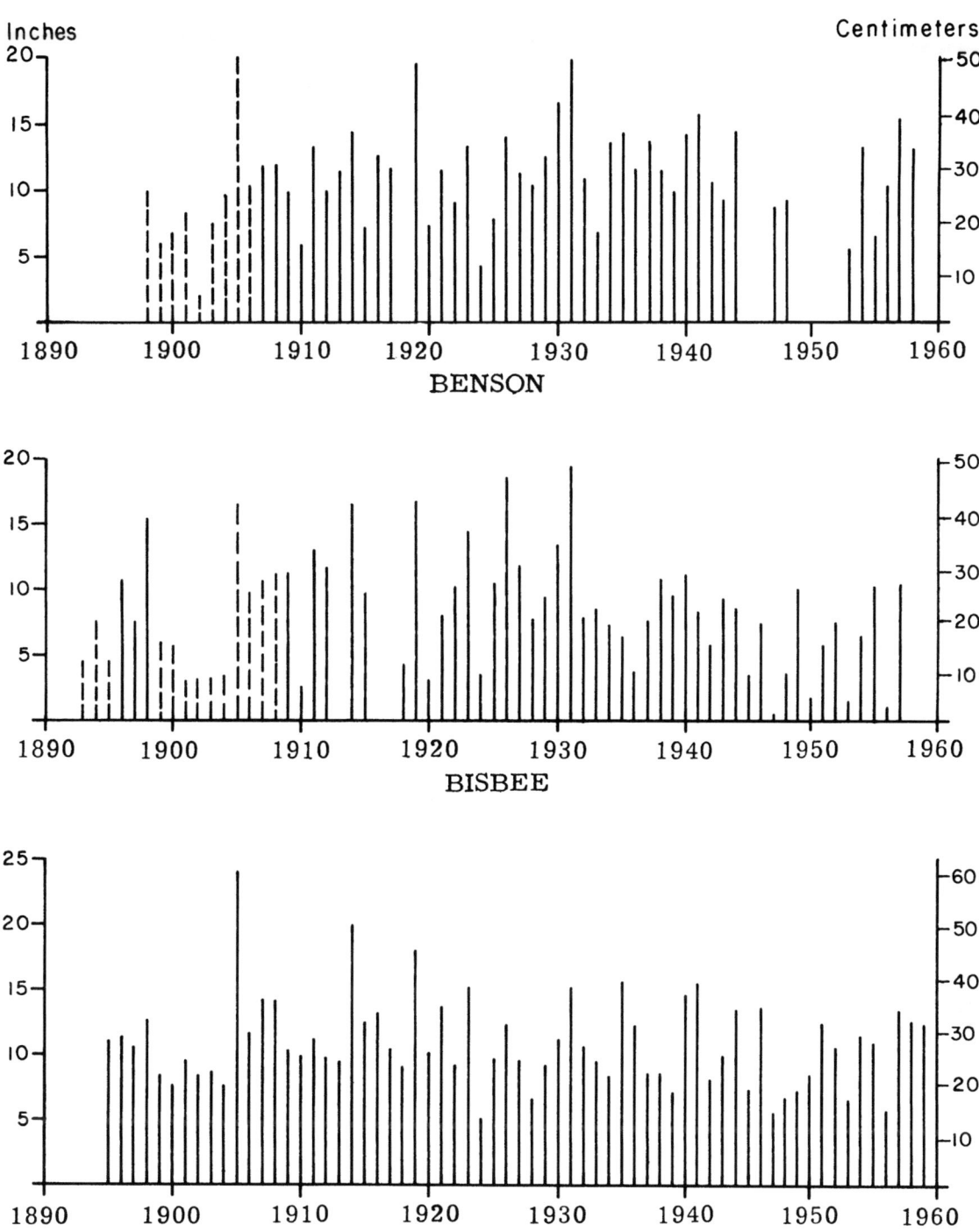

Figure 4.2. Annual precipitation plots from stations in southeastern Arizona showing the drought of 1892 to 1904 (compiled by the U.S. Weather Bureau; Sellers 1960).

that may have affected both runoff and vegetation. The unstable conditions resulted in the establishment of some new channels and the deposition of a small amount of coarse material by relatively fast-moving water. The inferred environmental instability does not seem to have been as great as that of the post-Unit 3 and pre-Unit 2 cutting for the following reasons: (1) the maximum depth of the channels is nearly equal for both periods of cutting, (2) some of the older stream courses were maintained, (3) deposition was not interrupted in the nearby parts of the floodplain, and (4) only a few of the cienegas were drained (Fig. 4.1c). After the channels were cut, conditions became somewhat more stabilized, as evidenced by intermittent extension of the swampy areas (where Unit 4 sediments were deposited) and the restriction of the fluvial sediments of Unit 3 mainly to the eastern part of Cienega Valley. Sometime after A.D.

900, relatively coarse material was deposited by streams over all of Cienega Valley. Thus, partly by filling and partly by draining, the cienegas disappeared. The stream courses were not stabilized and a large amount of sand and gravel was deposited. Some of these deposits are similar to those of Unit 1 laid down prior to the present arroyo cutting. This type of deposition, chiefly scour-and-fill, indicates rather rapid and sporadic runoff suggestive of unstable environmental conditions.

POLLEN PROFILE FROM THE EAST BANK OF CIENEGA CREEK

Paul S. Martin

Floodplain deposits in the Southwest have been of utmost importance to the prehistorian and paleoecologist. Exposed in arroyos dissecting the floodplain are the cultural debris of prehistoric man and assorted fossil remains preserved during the postglacial period. The arroyo walls also provide ready access to the fossil pollen record of the floodplain deposits.

A pollen profile was collected from the cleaned vertical east bank of the Cienega Creek arroyo. This locality is about 152 m east of the western border of the floodplain and upstream from measured Section MC–6. Ten to fifty grams of sediments were collected at 10 cm intervals to a depth of 6.7 m, the present bed of Cienega Creek. As shown in Figure 4.3, sufficient pollen was recovered for 200 grain counts at 28 levels.

Extraction proceeded according to the HF method by Faegri and Iversen (1950: 62), with the addition of a tetrabromethane flotation to aid in removal of colloid-forming silicates. The residue was mounted unstained on glass slides in poppy seed oil.

The pollen profile was collected 136 m upstream from Section MC–6; some of the subunit boundaries do not agree precisely with those at MC–6, although the larger subunits occur in both localities. The contact between Unit 3 and the Sanford formation is arbitrary and occupies a zone over 30.5 cm wide. These discrepancies in the stratigraphic column do not seriously affect the age interpretation.

The dominant pollen types are anemophilous herbaceous plants of the families Chenopodiaceae, Compositae, and Gramineae. Periporate pollen grains may represent any of the genera of Chenopodiaceae plus the related genus *Amaranthus*. The composites include mainly small, low-spined grains of the tribe Ambrosieae. Large-spined entomophilous composite grains are present but less common. Sedge (Cyperaceae) pollen appeared most frequently in dark, organic muds laid down in cienegas (floodplain marshes; Martin, Schoenwetter, and Arms 1961, pl. 2). *Typha*, a reliable indicator of ponding and shallow eutrophic lakes, was not found.

The chenopod-amaranths, wind-pollinated composites, and sedges achieve their best growth on floodplains. They have smaller populations on the grass-dominated uplands. The high percentage of grass pollen in two cattle tanks located on slopes near the floodplain should reflect closely the regional pollen rain where it is uninfluenced by the floodplain community (Martin, Schoenwetter, and Arms 1961, pls. 3, 4). It is essential to recognize that the pollen profile "overrepresents" this last element. The pollen profile does not necessarily reveal changes in upland vegetation (grama grassland) at any period. The only grassland species definitely not part of the floodplain community is Mormon tea (*Ephedra trifurca*). Although it is not abundant, *Ephedra* grows within 909 m of the pollen section.

The scarcity of mesquite (*Prosopis*) pollen, now the dominant tree on the Cienega Creek floodplain, is notable. Mesquite pollen was detected in a few samples examined from Section MC–5, but apparently its presence as a microfossil is erratic, a condition typical of insect-pollinated plants. Although mesquite grows immediately adjacent to the Cienega and Empire ranch cattle tanks, it contributes only one or two percent to their pollen sum. Mesquite pollen was more abundant in a cow dung sample (Fig. 4.3). Because mesquite is a favorite browse of cattle, this is not surprising.

The occurrence of oak and pine pollen represents transport from more distant sources. Oak is abundant above 1667 m, the nearest site (Martin, Schoenwetter, and Arms 1961, pl. 1). Twelve percent of oak pollen appeared in the Empire ranch cattle tank, reflecting the proximity of a stand of Emory oak in Gardner Canyon, within a mile of the tank.

Pine is more remote; a distance of some 22.5 km separates the site from the lower boundary of pinyon (*Pinus cembroides*) in the Santa Rita Mountains. Elevations above 1667 m in the Santa Rita Mountains are occupied by *Pinus ponderosa*, *P. leiophylla*, *P. engelmanni*, and *P. reflexa*. Presence of both large and small pine pollen grains indicates that both pinyon and some of the high elevation species contributed pollen to the floodplain sediments. No fir pollen was recovered, although white fir (*Abies concolor*) and Douglas fir (*Pseudotsuga taxifolia*) occupy upper forest zones of the Santa Rita Mountains.

The pollen diagram (Fig. 4.3) features one major change (Martin, Schoenwetter, and Arms 1961: 50–53, fig. 17), the "chenopod-composite" shift occurring between Levels 109 and 120 or between Unit 3 and the deposition of the Sanford formation. The dominant pollen types in deeper sediments are composites of the Ambrosieae; at Level 120 and above, the chenopod-amaranth group dominates. Although this shift cannot be dated precisely, it seems to have occurred before the period of arroyo cutting in the twelfth and thirteenth centuries A.D. and during the deposition of the upper part of Unit 3, which contains remains of the Sedentary period, A.D. 900 to 1200. The climatic meaning of the chenopod-composite shift is a matter of speculation.

From the viewpoint of the prehistorian, the presence of maize (*Zea*) is noteworthy. The monoporate graminoid grains larger than 70 u probably belong to this genus or its hybrid, Teosinte (compare Barghoorn, Wolfe, and Clisby 1954). In Level 190 clusters of maize grains constituted 99 percent of the pollen present. It seems probable that this field site was under cultivation during the Sedentary period of the Hohokam culture when the deposition of the upper part of Unit 3 occurred. Maize pollen also appeared at two other levels in Unit 3. Because the unit dates within the ceramic period at this locality, the presence of maize is not

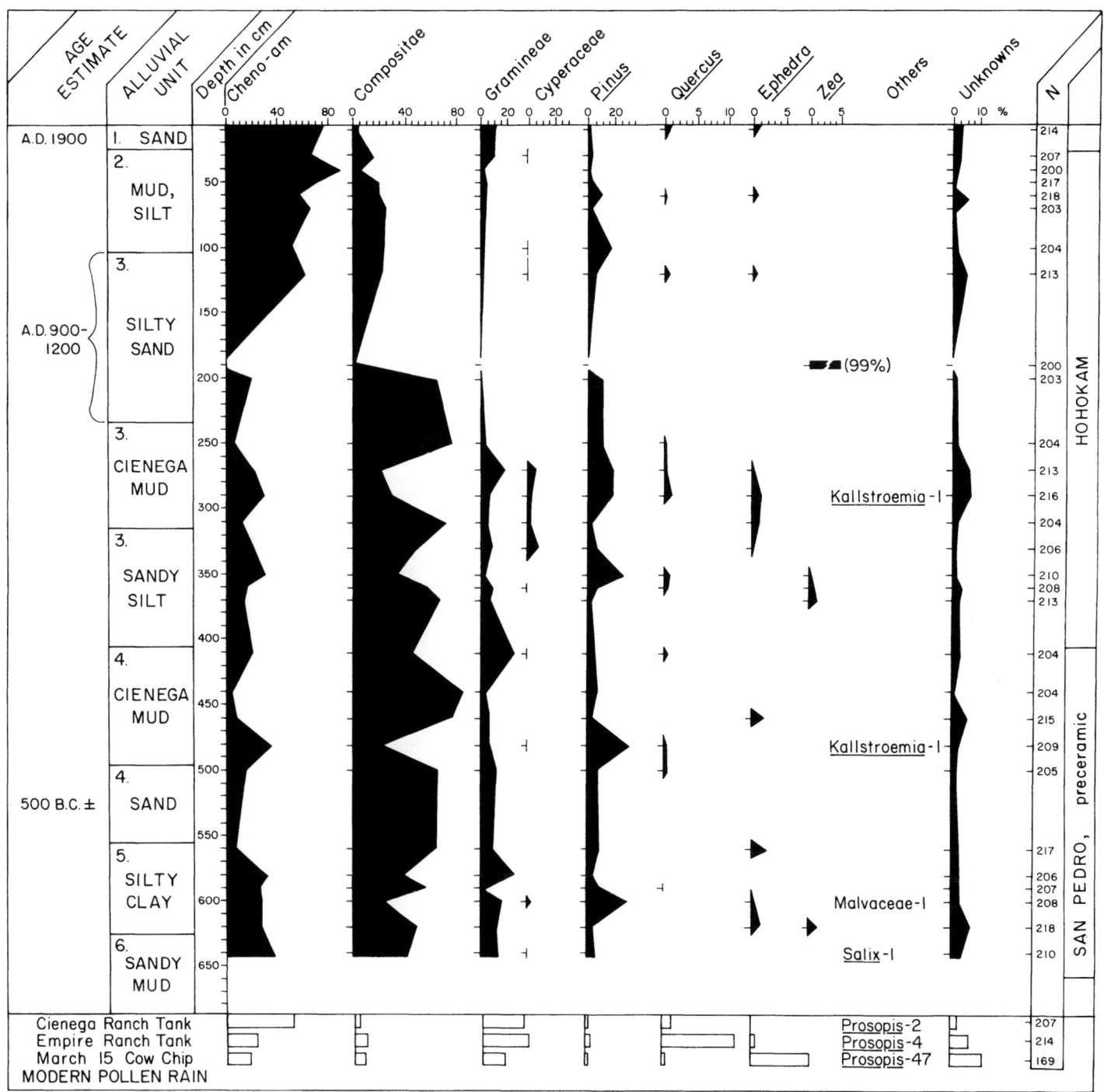

Figure 4.3. Pollen profile from Cienega Creek near Section MC–6 (from Martin 1963, fig. 17).

unexpected. On the other hand, three grains appeared at Level 620 at Unit 5, a unit definitely within the San Pedro stage of occupation, and this record adds to the evidence of prepottery *Zea* in the Southwest.

In summary, the following features characterize the Cienega Creek pollen diagram (Fig. 4.3).

1. The dominant pollen types are of nonarboreal species.
2. The sediments are fluviatile and, compared with basin sediments in regions of subdued relief, there is a greater possibility of allogenic pollen being carried into the deposit from some distant source. Good preservation of the fossil pollen grains and the general type of depositional environment, however, suggest that this is not a serious problem and that most pollen is not redeposited.
3. In comparing the fossil percentages with those obtained from recent cattle tank samples, there is a strong indication that the profile overrepresents pollen from vegetation growing on the floodplain.

4. The time span is short, and the entire depositional sequence of 6.7 m falls within the Sub-Atlantic and Sub-Boreal periods of the European chronology, or Zones C–2 and C–3 (oak-hickory, oak-chestnut) as generally recognized in the eastern United States (Deevey and Flint 1957).

5. A major pollen shift appears after the tenth century, a time of little change in pollen diagrams from the north temperate region.

6. Pollen of *Zea* occurs in both ceramic and preceramic cultural deposits.

WOOD IDENTIFICATION

Charcoal samples obtained from cooking pits at Arizona EE:2:30 and EE:2:35 (San Pedro stage sites) were identified as oak and mesquite (see Table 2.1) before reduction to elemental carbon by the University of Arizona Radiocarbon Laboratory. Firewood brought into camp by San Pedro stage people is assumed to reflect the most readily available fuel in the area, likely trees growing within a mile of the campsites. At this time, mesquite probably grew on the floodplain and on the lower parts of the adjacent ridges, while oak grew along drainages on the slopes of the ridges.

No mesquite or oak was identified at Arizona EE:2:34, which was occupied during the Colonial period. The wood recovered from this site was used in the construction of a pit house, and the selection of beams from ash, cottonwood, willow, juniper, and pine(?) was probably due to the usability of these woods. Although these beams may have been transported long distances, more likely these tree species were growing along drainages and lows on the floodplain; with the exception of juniper and pine, these trees are found in the area today.

FRESHWATER AND LAND INVERTEBRATES

Freshwater and land invertebrates collected from the alluvium of Units 1 through 5 and 7 (Table 4.1) were identified by Robert J. Drake (1958a, b). The shell remains were collected from soils and cienega deposits composed of sediments deposited in or near swamps. In most of the samples, land snail material appeared to be from grassland or moderate vegetation cover, whereas freshwater molluscs from 13 of the 14 samples were from shallow water habitats.

Many gastropods are indicators of temperature as well as habitat, and, if collected in sufficient numbers, can aid in the interpretation of past environments and climates. Unfortunately, the collection in Cienega Valley was not sufficiently comprehensive to warrant climatic interpretation. In general, however, the collection indicated a moist environment, which is confirmed by the high organic content and sedimentary features of the beds containing the invertebrates.

MAMMALS

Based on the present environment and on mammals identified from bone specimens obtained at the San Pedro stage site of Arizona EE:2:30 (see Table 2.2), it seems likely that

TABLE 4.1
Distribution of Freshwater and Land Invertebrates from Recent Alluvial Units in Cienega Valley

Invertebrates*	Alluvial Units						
	1	2	3	4	5	6	7
PELECYPODS							
Freshwater							
Pisidium sp.	X	X	X		X		
GASTROPODS							
Freshwater							
Amnicolids		X					X
Helisoma sp.	X	X	X				
Lymnaea sp.		X					
Physa sp.		X					
Land							
Cionella sp.					X		
Gastrocopta sp.			X	X			X
Hawaiia sp.	X	X	X		X		
Pupilla sp.	X						
Pupoides sp.							X
Succineids	X	X	X	X	X		
Vertigo sp.		X	X				

*Identified by Robert J. Drake.
X indicates present.

San Pedro man hunted game in three general vegetation habitats: grassland, mixed grassland-shrub, and woodland-forest (see Fig. 1.4). The principal game animals represented are antelope (31 bones), mule deer (55 bones), and jackrabbit (25 bones). Because antelope are restricted mainly to grazing on grasslands, the number of antelope bones recovered through excavation means that grassland cover may have been as extensive during the San Pedro stage as it is now. An association of mule deer, cottontail, and jackrabbit indicates a mixed grassland-shrub habitat. Mule deer are browsers, requiring a shrub environment like the kind found along a stream or dry watercourse. The greater number of mule deer bones in proportion to bones from other animals implies not only that this animal was an important prey during San Pedro times, but indirectly that it was of common occurrence. Jackrabbit and cottontail need a shrub and grass cover, while the pocket gopher (a single archaeological occurrence) requires grassland or streamside cover. Hunting in the oak-pine forest and woodland at higher altitudes in the nearby mountains is suggested by the identification of elk, bighorn sheep(?), and whitetail deer remains. In general, elk and bighorn sheep prefer a rough, mountainous terrain, but they sometimes feed at lower elevations. Whitetail deer range between oak and the higher pine forest. Because predatory animals such as bobcat and coyote range widely from the Sonoran desert to the high altitude pine forest, excavated bone remains of these animals have little paleoecological value.

COMPARISON OF DATA USED IN ENVIRONMENTAL INTERPRETATION

Reconstructions of past environments in the Cienega Valley are derived mainly from interpretations of the alluvial deposits and the pollen contained in the alluvium. Other data from the freshwater and land invertebrates, wood, and mammal remains found in the archaeological sites are fragmentary, and therefore have limited use in environmental interpretation. Historical evidence has a short time span, so it, too, is restrictive. Thus, the discussion of past environments is based largely on the information gained from analyses of pollen obtained at two locations—near Section MC–6 (see Fig. 4.3) and at Section MC–5 (Schoenwetter 1960, fig. 1)—and from the alluvial stratigraphy studied in detail at Sections MC–1 through MC–7, mapped from the arroyo walls of Matty Wash and Cienega Creek.

Fossil pollen grains occurring in the alluvial deposits have a complex history. Pollen is unique not only because of its abundance and size, but also because it is an organic substance that can be classified as a sediment. Favorable conditions for the accumulation and preservation of pollen are generally found in silts, muds, and clays laid down in quiet water.

The four depositional environments that are present in Cienega Valley—classified as lacustrine, cienega, soil forming, and fluvial—have different characteristics affecting the entrapment and preservation of pollen. Pollen enclosed in lacustrine sediments may be derived from vegetation growing along the shore of a pond or lake. It may also be transported into the lake by streams or carried in the wind and deposited on the surface of the lake. A cienega contains little open water and occupies areas not affected by streams except in flooding. The pollen in cienegas, then, is more representative of airborne and local sources. Likewise, a soil may form only in areas not affected by scouring and deposition by streams or flooding by lakes. However, the upper part of a buried soil, containing pollen that may differ from that in the adjacent deposits, is commonly removed by erosion that occurs before the deposition of the overlying deposits. In this kind of situation, an environmental change is indicated by remnants of the soil in the alluvial sequence, but such change may not be recognized in the pollen record.

Fluvial environments present complex problems with regard to deposition of pollen: (1) currents depositing sand and gravel tend to carry in suspension the finer materials, including pollen, and may move them out of the area; (2) coarse detritus transported by streams tends to crush and maul all finer grained materials; (3) scour-and-fill action with redeposition of all older deposits containing pollen tends to contaminate the pollen record; and (4) many of the fluvial-laid sediments have been subjected to alternating wetting and drying, usually after oxidizing conditions that often destroy pollen.

Disturbances in local and regional environments are recorded by both the alluvial stratigraphy and the pollen record. Slight differences in the depositional environment of the cienega sediments are indicated by alternating lithologies of muds to sandy silts, thickness of beds, and amounts of carbonaceous material preserved. The pollen recorded from these sedimentary deposits reveals a series of minor fluctuations among the chenopod-amaranths and composites. Differences in the depositional environments of fluvial sediments are indicated by lithologic changes from silt to gravel; by lenticularity of the beds; and by the amount, size, and distribution of channels; and they are reflected in the pollen record by perhaps larger shifts of the composites and chenopod-amaranths than are generally reflected in cienega deposits. Unfortunately, there are large gaps in the pollen record, because the extraction of pollen from sandy and gravelly fluvial sediments is difficult or pollen is absent. Major shifts of the chenopod-amaranths and composites seem to have occurred near the contact of the cienega deposits with the fluvial sediments. These shifts are seen in Unit 3A (Appendix B) that overlies cienega deposits, in the profile near Section MC–6, and in Unit 1 overlying cienega deposits of Unit 2 at Section MC–5 (Figs. 2.16, 4.3). If there were no gaps in the pollen record at Section MC–5, other major shifts would probably be indicated near the contacts of Units 3B and 3A with Unit 2 (Appendix A).

In general, pine (*Pinus*) and, to a lesser extent, oak (*Quercus*) are present in a relatively higher percentage in the cienega beds and soil zones—deposits that accumulate slowly in areas away from the influence of streams—than in fluvial-laid sediments. More than 5 percent of pine pollen is present in the muds of Unit 6. More than 15 percent of oak and pine pollen is represented in the peaty deposits of the M_1 marker bed and the underlying deposits in the lower part of Unit 3, in the K marker bed in the middle part of Unit 3, and in Unit 2 (the Sanford formation). The high percentage of pine and oak pollen may be the result of the slow deposition rates of these sediments that allowed a greater amount of airborne pollen to be represented or the result of a slight environmental fluctuation.

Cyperaceae pollen occurs in significant amounts in the part of Unit 3 located below the M_1 marker bed at Section MC–5 and in the K marker bed at Section MC–6. These sediments reflect a wet depositional environment favorable for the growth of sedges, although no cyperaceae pollen was extracted from other deposits of the area (such as Units 4 and 6) that had similar depositional environments.

In summary, there seems to be an association of composites, pine, and oak with the fine sediments deposited in cienegas, ponds, and soils, and an association of chenopod-amaranths with the generally coarse fluvial-laid sediments. Large gaps in the pollen record, where pollen has not been preserved or extracted, coincide with the fluvial deposits. In Cienega Valley the pollen is confined mainly to sediments deposited in cienega and lacustrine environments and to soils, while the fluvial-laid sediments, forming roughly half of the alluvium, contain only scanty pollen remains.

5. CULTURAL AND ENVIRONMENTAL HISTORY

Cultural history in Cienega Valley begins with the San Pedro stage of the Cochise culture at a time when the general environmental conditions were becoming more favorable for semipermanent occupation. Although there is little evidence of human activity before 1000 B.C. in Cienega Valley, earlier stages of the Cochise culture have been described for southern Arizona (Sayles and Antevs 1941; Sayles 1983) and Ventana Cave (Haury 1950). The presence of perennial water in the area today during a period of drought (Thomas 1963) suggests that at least some water was available during the relatively dry period of the early Recent, termed the Altithermal period by Antevs (1955), and that people could have been in the valley before the San Pedro stage. A sidescraper (Fig 2.1 a) found in Unit 7 at Arizona EE:2:12 (Fig. 5.1) may possibly be from a pre-San Pedro occupation. A radiocarbon date of approximately 1500 B.C. was obtained from Unit 7, where the sidescraper was found.

Evidence of sites older than the San Pedro stage is limited by the exposures uncovered through arroyo cutting and the amount of erosion that occurred in all of Recent time. The basal part of the late Recent alluvium may have been laid down in a depositional environment similar to that of the San Pedro stage and may thus contain older, but still concealed, sites. Localities that were occupied before the deposition of the late Recent alluvium sequence probably have been subjected to vigorous erosion during the early Recent and, consequently, many sites may have been destroyed. Also, much of the evidence for sites in the upland areas adjoining Cienega Valley may have been removed by erosion occurring there throughout Recent time.

EARLY SAN PEDRO STAGE

San Pedro stage sites, found buried on sandbars (mainly Unit 5) and slopes adjacent to the ancient floodplain, represent semipermanent and temporary campsites. The distribution of the sites shows a close association with cienegas and ponds of the old floodplain (see Fig. 4.1 a). The sedimentary features of Units 4, 5, and 6, and the pollen record, indicate that no major environmental change affected Cienega Valley during the San Pedro stage. The environment was stable, with enough moisture for the cienegas and for a grassland and shrub cover on the nearby uplands. Oak and grass covered most of the gravel terraces. Mesquite, identified from charcoal specimens (see Table 2.1), probably grew on the terraces or on lowlands bordering the floodplain, as well as on the floodplain itself. The pollen record near Section MC–6 shows plants often called weeds, composites and chenopod-amaranths, were the dominant types represented in the deposits of Units 4, 5, and 6.

Faunal remains excavated from San Pedro stage sites indicate the presence of animals similar to those of modern times. The grassland supported antelope; grassland and shrub cover supported mule deer, cottontail, and jackrabbit; and the forests of the nearby mountains supported elk, bighorn sheep, and whitetail deer.

The general environment produced excellent conditions for plant gathering and small game hunting for the San Pedro people. Recovered artifacts were undoubtedly used for gathering and hunting activities. The stone grinding and pounding tools imply the use of seeds, nuts, and berries for food. Cutting, scraping, and chopping activities were undoubtedly used in the skinning and preparation of animals. Some animals may have been cooked in deep earth-oven pits like those found at Arizona EE:2:30.

Maize pollen extracted from Units 4 and 6 near Section MC–6 (see Fig. 4.3) strongly suggests that part of the San Pedro subsistence pattern was based on maize cultivation. Corn probably was planted in areas bordering cienegas where little flooding occurred. Farming may have been limited to the floodplain where soil moisture was maintained by a shallow water table. The nearby uplands were undergoing erosion, which limited soil formation, and, consequently, farming.

The occupation of the site at Arizona EE:2:30 was concurrent with the formation of some of the peaty beds, representing deposition in cienegas, at Section MC–5 (see Fig 4.1 a). The midden at the site underlies Unit 3 and unconformably overlies Unit 100. The midden dips at a slightly steeper angle than the M_1 and M_2 marker beds. The M_1 marker bed is younger than the M_2 marker bed, but M_2 may be equivalent to the upper part of the midden. The marshes represented by the deposition of the peaty sediments below this marker bed at Section MC–5 and of Unit 4 sediments elsewhere in Cienega Valley were concurrent with the habitation at Arizona EE:2:30 and likely were exploited for edible marsh plants (Fig. 5.1).

Population during the San Pedro stage was probably fairly small compared with later periods, but such evidence is scanty because most sites were buried by more than 3 m of alluvium. An important cultural feature is the indicated stability of the local group that occupied Arizona EE:2:30. The large number of pits, the extensive midden, flexed human burials, and the pit houses at Arizona EE:2:30 all evince a semisettled way of life that provided the logical transition to true village communities and agriculturalism of later times. The other sites of this period represent only temporary camps, which may have been used by groups operating out of a base camp at Arizona EE:2:30.

LATE SAN PEDRO STAGE AND EARLY PIONEER PERIOD

The addition of pottery to the San Pedro stage cultural inventory marks the transition to the early Pioneer Hohokam culture. Pit houses were the characteristic habitation unit of the Pioneer period. Except for pit houses and ceramics, there was little change in the material culture from that of the early San Pedro stage. Although evidence is scarce for this period, subsistence techniques were probably similar to those of the preceding San Pedro stage.

The proximity of a Vahki-Estrella dated site (Arizona EE:2:10) to a San Pedro stage site (Arizona EE:2:30), and the midden at the base of Unit 3 alluvium between the two sites, possibly reflect a continuous occupation of the area. Fluvial-laid material mixed with the midden indicates that early Unit 3 deposition was concurrent with the occupation of the pit house at Arizona EE:2:10. Unit 3 deposits overlapped eastward on the prealluvial valley floor and buried the older San Pedro sites (including Arizona EE:2:30), but Arizona EE:2:10 may have been along the margin of the alluvial floodplain and consequently was not buried until later.

In general, the environmental conditions of the early Pioneer period were similar to those of the San Pedro stage. Cienegas continued to occur in the western and central parts of the floodplain (see Table 3.2). Although influxes of Unit 3 fluvial sediments came from both sides of the valley, the areas occupied by the cienegas shifted slightly. The M_1 marker bed at Section MC-5 was formed as a result of one of the eastward shifts of cienega deposition. If the M_1 marker bed were projected from Section MC-5 to Arizona EE:2:10, it would occupy a stratigraphic position near or at the base of Unit 3 in the area of the pit house. Thus, this cienega was also available for the collection of edible marsh plants during early Pioneer period times (Fig. 4.1 b).

LATE PIONEER PERIOD

Near the beginning of the late Pioneer period, the cienegas began to dwindle. With the encroachment of fluvial-laid materials, the cienegas were restricted to the southwestern part and several small areas in the eastern part of the valley. The shrinkage of the cienegas and the enlargement of the alluvial floodplain added to the potential farming area of Cienega Valley throughout the Pioneer period. A probable shift in environmental conditions caused the formation of an apparently integrated system of channels (see Fig. 4.1 c) between about A.D. 200 to 300 and A.D. 600. The channeling was not deep enough to drain the cienegas, thereby not appreciably affecting maize agriculture. The recording of maize pollen in sediments deposited at this time near Section MC-6 supports the inference that conditions were suitable for growing maize. In addition, the pollen record (see Fig. 4.3) indicates no significant environmental change during this time, mainly because both profiles are in areas not affected by the channeling. After the channels were cut, filling took place. The cienegas were enlarged locally, but were restricted chiefly to the west side of the valley.

The deposition of alluvium over all the lowlands may have influenced the occupation of ridges adjoining the floodplain. Occupation of ridge localities in the valley is noted for the first time at Arizona EE:2:40. The occupation at Arizona EE:2:10 continued as the alluvial deposits were extended throughout Cienega Valley (Fig. 5.1).

COLONIAL AND SEDENTARY PERIODS

Throughout the Colonial and Sedentary periods the environmental conditions, except perhaps during the deposition of the K marker bed (see Fig. 4.1d), were generally unstable compared with the preceding periods. Fluvial material, mainly from Matty Wash, was laid down on most of the floodplain; consequently, many of the cienegas were filled. The deposition of the K marker bed indicates a temporary expansion of the cienegas. After the deposition of the K marker bed, the alluvial deposits reflect a shift in environmental conditions. Scour-and-fill became the dominant sedimentary process and fluvial sediments were deposited throughout Cienega Valley. A shift in the environmental conditions is indicated by an abrupt increase of chenopod-amaranths and a decrease of composites recorded in the pollen profile near Section MC-6 (see Fig. 4.3). This change in the pollen took place near the Unit 3 and Unit 4 contact, and it nearly coincides with the change from cienega (Unit 4) to fluvial deposition (Unit 3). Because no pollen was extracted from the corresponding stratigraphic interval in upper Unit 3, this pollen shift was not substantiated in the profile at Section MC-5.

The fluvial deposition that occurred throughout the valley during the Sedentary period and, to a lesser extent, the Colonial period, probably increased the effective farming area on the floodplain. A pollen sample obtained from the upper part of Unit 3 near Section MC-6, deposited during this time, yielded 99 percent maize pollen. This unusual record provides evidence of a cornfield in an area previously occupied by a cienega.

Sites of the Colonial and Sedentary periods are found on the floodplain and on adjacent ridges (see Figs. 1.3, 4.1d). For these periods population increase is inferred from the number of villages surveyed on the terraces and the widespread distribution of sites on the floodplain. The population may have reached a maximum during the Sedentary period, and may have continued through the early Classic at this peak.

CLASSIC PERIOD

The environmental conditions of Cienega Valley during the late part of the Sedentary period and the early part of the Classic were probably similar. At some time during this interval, however, fluvial deposition probably ceased, followed by stripping and eventually arroyo cutting (Fig. 5.1). The arroyos represent only the end stage of this erosional

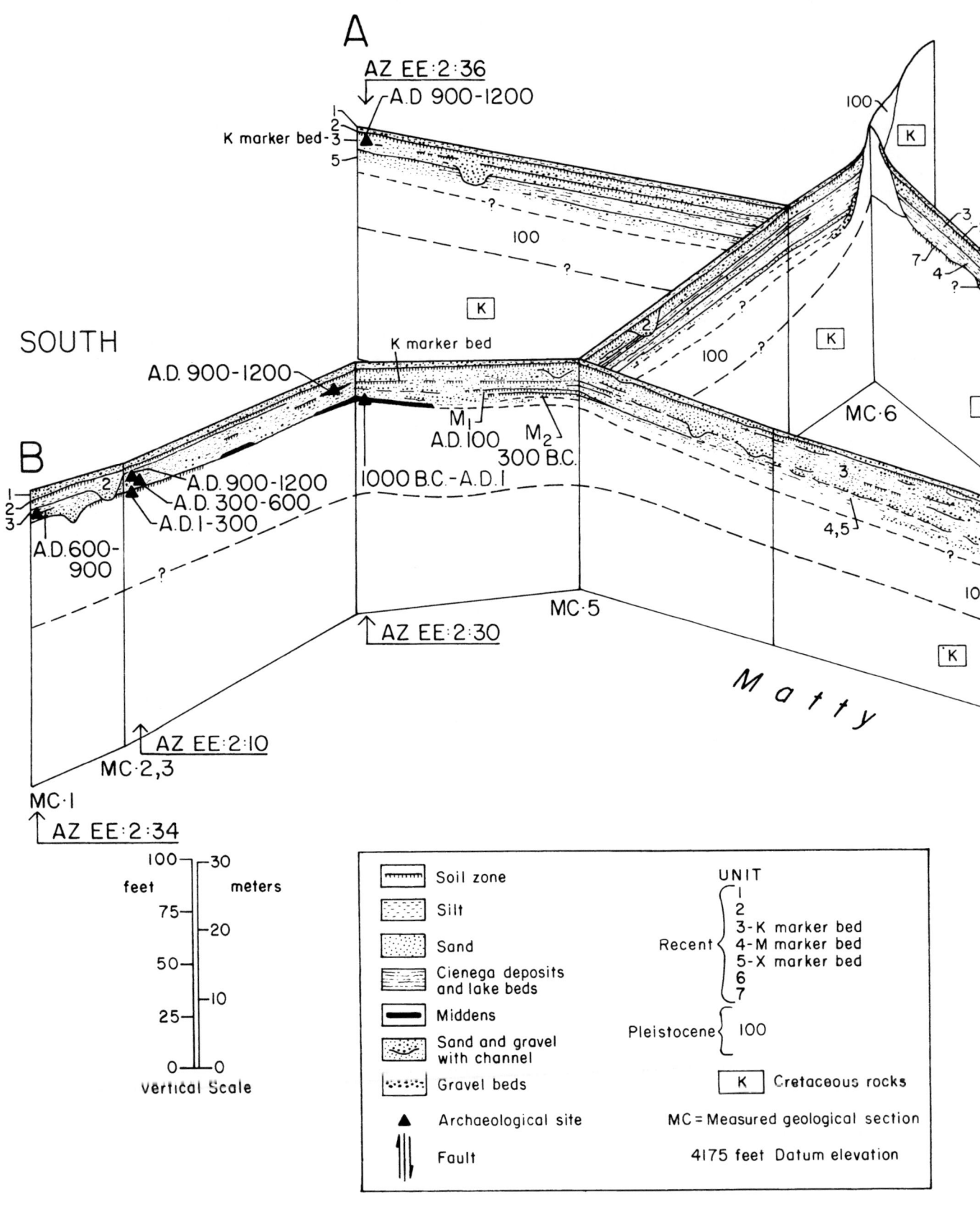

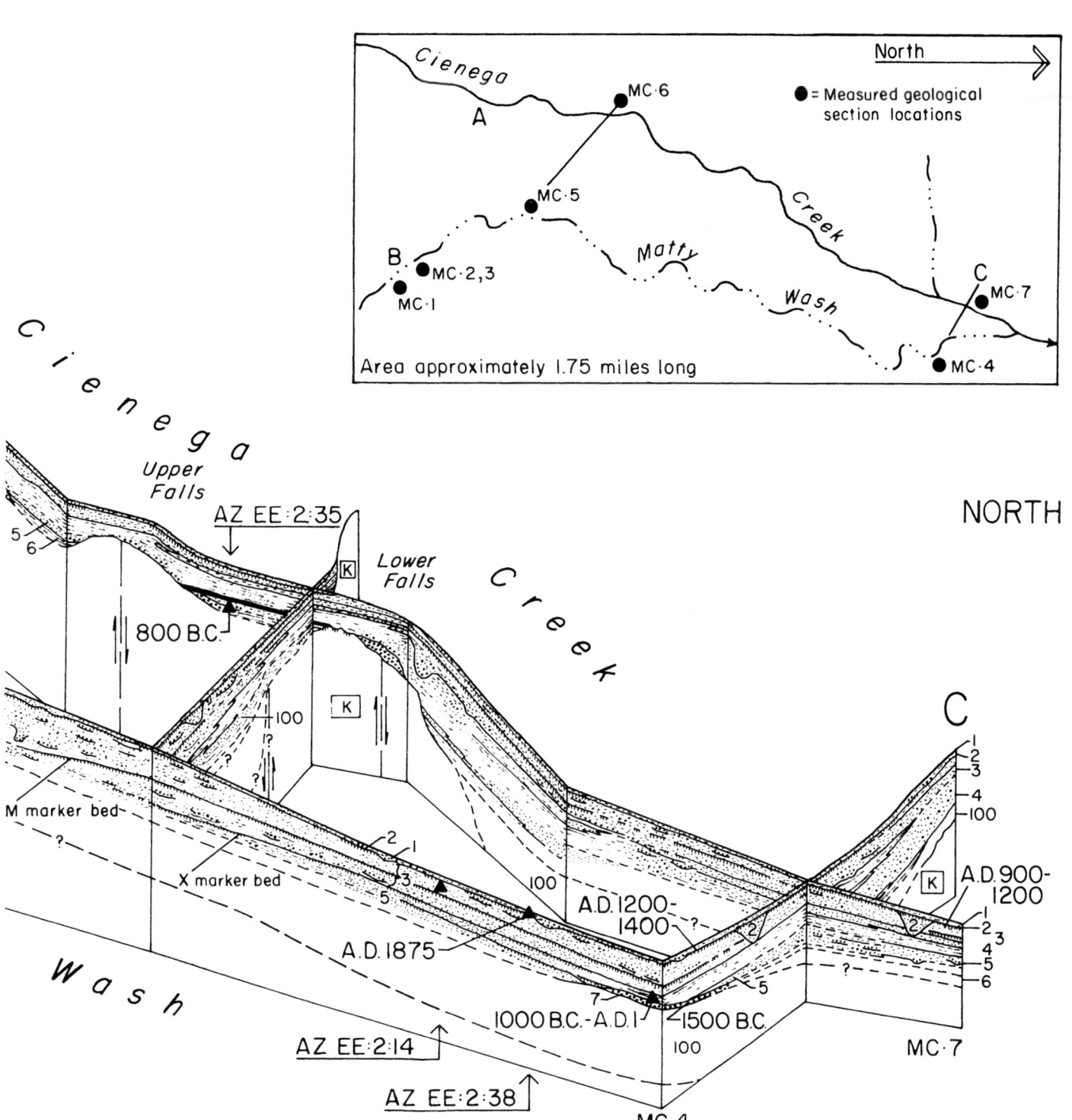

Figure 5.1. Isometric fence diagram of Cienega Valley, Arizona, illustrating Recent alluvial stratigraphic relationships.

interval. Conditions favoring erosion were caused by an unstable environment, in turn reflecting an unstable climate. Precipitation must have been particularly unreliable, with fluctuations similar to modern southeastern Arizona (see Figs. 2.16, 4.2). The effects of the inferred drought of the late Sedentary and early Classic periods, often referred to as the Great Drought, may not have been as severe as present effects because the arroyos at that time were smaller and had a more limited distribution than the modern ones (Fig. 4.1 *b*).

Archaeological controls were insufficient to determine how the local inhabitants adapted to this changing environment or whether they abandoned the area because of the drought and arroyo cutting. In any event, some modification in floodplain cultivation methods (Hack 1942: 29) must have been necessary near the newly formed arroyos. Based on three main factors, occupation appears to have been continuous until A.D. 1300. First, most ridge sites occupied during the Sedentary period also contained early Classic remains. Second, not all of the floodplain was affected by arroyo trenching. No arroyo extended upstream along Cienega Creek south of the area investigated, and floodplain farming could have been practiced there without interruption. Third, the permanent water supply in Cienega Valley today indicates that an adequate supply would have been available in the area during this period.

As drought conditions abated, perhaps during the middle Classic period, the environment stabilized and precipitation became more reliable. Less environmental fluctuation is reflected in the fine-grained sediments and soil of Unit 2, the Sanford formation. During the late Classic, streamflow was sluggish, and cienegas were present on parts of the floodplain until they were destroyed by arroyo cutting that began in historical times.

Pollen evidence of maize agriculture during the Classic period is absent, but the size and number of villages of the Tanque Verde phase denote its continuance. Population, as measured by the number of villages, continued through the early Classic period (Tanque Verde phase) with the same relative size as during the previous Sedentary period; for the late Classic, only one site was located dating to the Tucson phase.

The cause of the population decline and eventual abandonment of Cienega Valley is not known from the available information. Although the effects of arroyo cutting and filling of the cienegas on the areas of occupation are uncertain, these sharp differences in environmental conditions must have had a strong influence on the Classic period occupation.

DISCUSSION

Environmental conditions before about A.D. 300 were generally stable; those after A.D. 300 showed considerable fluctuation. Continuity appears in the similarity of life forms three thousand years ago compared with those observed in Cienega Valley today. Fluctuations in the environment are recorded in the alluvial stratigraphy and in the pollen records as changing conditions shifted the areas occupied by cienegas. The sedimentary pattern on the floodplain has been interrupted by influxes of fluvial deposits and twice by arroyo cutting (during the twelfth or thirteenth century and at present). The channels cut some time between A.D. 200 to 300 and 600 apparently had only a minor influence on the floodplain deposition.

To what extent the past environments of Cienega Valley influenced the development of prehistoric communities can only be inferred. The early cienega environments on the floodplain provided optimum conditions for plant gatherers and small game hunters. The continuity in chipped stone tools throughout the cultural sequence means that hunting and gathering were an integral part of the economy. The extent of the cienegas perhaps limited floodplain areas available for cultivation, in turn limiting the role of maize as a stable food in the total subsistence pattern. As the floodplain expanded through alluviation and the cienegas diminished, the area available for farming increased, and a corresponding rise in population occurred until a peak was reached in late Sedentary or early Classic times. Although the factors that caused the decline in population and abandonment of Cienega Valley in the Classic period cannot be determined with certainty, they probably were closely related to the sharp environmental changes that took place at that time.

Appendix A

STRATIGRAPHIC SECTION MC–5

Location: West bank of Matty Wash, 455 m northwest and downstream from site Arizona EE:2:10.

Unit	Thickness	
		RECENT
1	76.2 cm	Sand: pale brown 5YR–5/2 to light brown 5YR–6/4, silt to fine-grained sand, fair-sorted, subangular to angular; muscovite rare and black mineral common as accessories; very weakly cemented to uncemented, calcareous; splits crumbly; flat and lenticular thin-bedded; cross-bedded; lenticular; weathers smooth; forms regular slope; environment, quiet fluvial, floodplain, with some brown sand; base is sharp and flat.

Unconformity, erosional, prominent throughout area, relief of less than 30.5 cm.

2	30.5 cm	Silt: brownish-gray 5YR–4/1, silt to very fine-grained sand; muscovite rare and black mineral common as accessories; very weakly cemented, calcareous and argillaceous; structureless; splits crumbly and friable; weathers hackly; forms ledge; some columnar structure; small gastropod fossils; essentially a soil zone developed on Unit 3; environment, floodplain, a soil zone; base is indefinite.
3A	137.2 cm	Silty sand: pale red 10R–6/2, silt to fine-grained sand, poorly sorted, subrounded to angular; weakly cemented, calcareous; splits crumbly; flat and lenticular thin- to thick-bedded and structureless; cross-bedded, lenticular low angle, medium scale trough; weathers smooth; forms vertical ledge. Divided in descending order into the following parts:
		Structureless silty sand 61.0 cm
		Sand and gravel 30.5 cm
		Structureless silty sand 45.7 cm
		Contains whitish limy film throughout unit; gravel 12.7 cm maximum size; structureless units slightly columnar and jointed suggesting some loess deposition; limy encrustation on grains; environment, floodplain and alluvial fan, generally quiet fluvial; base is sharp and flat.
3B	61.0 cm	Sand silt: pale brown 5YR–5/2 to light brownish-gray 5YR–6/1, silt to fine-grained sand, poorly sorted, subangular; black mineral common as accessory; very weakly cemented, calcareous; splits friable; structureless; weathers into small blocks and hackly; forms part of ledge of Unit 3; two soil zones at section; grades laterally into one zone; ranges from 45.7 cm to 121.9 cm in thickness; contains small gastropod fossils; base is gradational.
3C	106.7 cm	Silty sand: pale brown 5YR–5/2, silt to fine-grained sand, subangular to angular; muscovite rare and black mineral common as accessories; very weakly cemented, calcareous and argillaceous; splits crumbly; structureless and partly flat-bedded; contains thin soil zone; some leaching at tip of unit; grades laterally into well-sorted sand 15.2 m to the north; contains small gastropod fossils; base is gradational.

3D	30.5 cm	Mud: brownish-gray 5YR–4/1, silt and clay with a few very fine sand grains; black mineral common as an accessory; very weakly cemented, calcareous; splits friable; flat and lenticular, very thin-bedded; weathers hackly; contains carbonaceous material. Unit consists in descending order of:

      Gray silty clay with peat   9.1 cm
      Silty sand, same as Unit 3C   9.1 cm
      Silt and peat   3.1 cm
      Silty sand, same as Unit 3C containing some peat   6.1 cm
      Silt and peat   3.1 cm

Forms the M_1 marker bed; base is gradational.

3E	61.0 cm	Silty sand: pale yellowish-brown 10YR–6/2 to grayish orange-pink 5YR–7/2, silt to very fine-grained sand with few fine grains; muscovite rare and black mineral common as accessories; weakly cemented, calcareous; splits crumbly; mudchips common; unit is alternation of silty sand same as Unit 3D with peaty silt; flat and lenticular, slightly crinkled, very thin-bedded; contains gastropod fossils; base is gradational.
3F	9.3 cm	Peat: dark gray N3 to medium light gray N6, very weakly cemented with peaty material, no calcareous material present; flat thin-bedded; beds within unit can be traced laterally for 30.3 m; unit thickens to 15.2 cm to the north; consists in descending order of:

      Peat   3.1 cm
      Gray silt   3.1 cm
      Peat   3.1 cm

Forms the M_2 marker bed; base is gradational.

3G	45.7 cm	Alternation of sandy silt and mud: medium light gray N6 to pale yellowish-brown 10YR–6/2, silt to fine-grained sand, subangular to angular; very weakly cemented, argillaceous; contains steaks of peaty silt; base is concealed.

Thickness (incomplete) of Unit 3: 4.5 m.

Appendix B

STRATIGRAPHIC SECTION MC–6

Location: In narrows about 311 m above lower falls on Cienega Creek.

Unit	Thickness	
		RECENT
1	30.5 cm	Sand: same as Unit 1 of Section MC–5 (Appendix A).

Unconformity, erosional, fairly flat, occurs throughout area.

2	15.2–91.4 cm	Mud: pale brown 5YR–5/2, silt and clay and a few fine and fine-grained sands; black mineral common as an accessory; very weakly cemented, calcareous; splits friable; structureless and thin- to thick-bedded; weathers hackly; forms irregular slope; environment, soil zone developed on a floodplain; base is indefinite and irregular.
3A	91.4–182.9 cm	Silty sand: light brownish-gray 5YR–6/1 to pale red 5R–6/2, silt to very fine-grained sand, poorly sorted, subangular to angular with few subrounded grains; black mineral common as an accessory; very weakly cemented, calcareous; splits massive, flat and lenticular thin- to thick-bedded; cross-bedded, lenticular, low to very low angle, small to medium scale trough; contains more channels filled with gravelly sand; few limy irregular-shaped inclusions; environment, generally quiet fluvial, floodplain; base is sharp and irregular with 15.3 cm relief.
3B	152.4 cm	Mud: medium gray N5, silt and clay with some very fine-grained sand; black mineral common as an accessory; very weakly cemented; calcareous; splits friable; structureless and very thin- to thin-bedded; weathers hackly; forms irregular slope or "niche;" environment, lacustrine or soil zone on floodplain; base is gradational.
3C	30.5 cm	Sand: pale brown 5YR–5/2 to light brown 5YR–6/4, silt to fine-grained sand with few medium grains, poorly sorted, subangular to angular with few subrounded grains; muscovite rare and black mineral common as accessories; very weakly cemented, calcareous; flat and lenticular thin-bedded; cross-bedded, lenticular low angle small- to medium-scale planer and trough; splits massive; weathers blocky; forms irregular ledge; becomes thicker to the north by intertonguing with Unit 4; more gravelly sand channels to the southeast; contains few very thin cienega beds and angular pebbles; environment, quiet fluvial, floodplain; base is partly gradational and partly sharp with 5.1 cm of relief.

Total thickness of Unit 3: 274.3–365.8 cm.

4	167.5 cm	Mud: brownish-gray 5YR–4/1 to pale brown 5YR–5/2, silt and clay with some very fine-grained sand; black mineral common as an accessory; very weakly cemented, calcareous; splits platy and shaley; flat and lenticular very thin-bedded; weathers hackly; forms irregular slope; contains few angular pebbles scattered throughout unit; contains small gastropod fossils and organic matter. Consists in descending order of:

Mud (cienega)	91.4 cm
Silty sand	15.2 cm
Mud (cienega)	15.2 cm
Sandy silt	15.2 cm
Mud (cienega)	30.5 cm

Environment, lacustrine and swamp; base is gradational.

5A	71.0 cm	Sand: pale yellowish-brown 10YR–6/2, very fine- to very coarse-grained, poorly sorted, subrounded to subangular; muscovite common and black mineral common as accessories; very weakly cemented, calcareous; splits crumbly; flat and lenticular thin-bedded; cross-bedded; lenticular low angle, small scale trough; weathers blocky; forms irregular ledge; coarser sand in small channel-like lenses; contains charcoal; magnetite(?) crystals embedded in quartz in one fragment; some small gravel; contains pink siltstone or silty sandstone fragments, subrounded; muscovite possibly altered to brown mineral; one hexagonal biotite crystal; environment, quiet fluvial; base is sharp and irregular with 15.2 cm of relief.
5B	76.2 cm	Silt and sandy silt: pale yellowish-brown 10YR–6/2 to light brownish-gray 5YR–6/1, clay to fine-grained sand; black mineral common as an accessory; very weakly cemented, calcareous; flat and lenticular very thin-bedded; weathers smooth; forms irregular slope; contains carbonaceous material; environment, quiet fluvial and ponding; base is both gradational and sharp and flat with less than 5.1 cm relief.
5C	0–15.2 cm	Sandy mud: brownish-gray 5YR–4/1, silt to medium-grained sand, poorly sorted, subangular to angular with few rounded to subrounded grains; black mineral common as an accessory; very weakly cemented, calcareous; structureless and thin-bedded; weathers hackly; forms ledge; contains few small pebbles and small gastropod fossils; slightly plastic when wet; grades laterally into basal part of Unit 5B; environment, quiet fluvial and partly residual or slight reworking of Unit 7; base is gradational.

Total thickness of Unit 5: 147.2–162.4 cm.

6	30.5 cm	Mud: clay and silt with some very fine and fine-grained sand; muscovite rare to common as an accessory; very weakly cemented, calcareous; structureless and thin-bedded; weathers blocky; splits shaley; forms irregular ledge; plastic when wet; environment, lacustrine; base is concealed.
7	16.2-91.4 cm	Pebbly silt: pale brown 5YR–4/2 to brownish-gray 5YR–4/1, clay to very coarse-grained sand, poorly sorted, subrounded to angular; black mineral common as an accessory; weakly cemented, calcareous; splits crumbly; structureless; weathers hackly; forms irregular ledge and slope; contains angular pebbles derived from Units 100 and 1000; Units 3A, 4, 5, and 6(?) intertongue with Unit 7; occupies depressions on Units 100 and 1000; environment, residual or soil; base is indefinite, sharp, and irregular.

Thickness (incomplete) of Recent deposits: 762+ cm.

PLEISTOCENE AND RECENT

Unconformity, erosional, forms prealluvial surface underlying the Recent deposits.

100	15+ m	Conglomerate: pale red 10R–6/2, to grayish orange-pink 5YR–7/2, very fine- to very coarse-grained, poorly sorted, subrounded to subangular with few rounded grains; black mineral common as an accessory; weakly cemented; calcareous; splits massive; lenticular thin- to thick-bedded; cross-bedded; lenticular low to very low angle, medium- to very large-scale trough; weathers round and hackly; forms irregular ledge and slope; gravel maximum size 30.5 cm, generally concentrated in broad lenses or wide channels; some caliche; upper 4.6 m on west side of Cienenga Creek weathered to shades of gray; few mudchips in very thin silt beds; environment, quiet and torrential fluvial, partly residual; base is sharp and irregular.

CRETACEOUS TO PLEISTOCENE(?)

Unconformity, erosional; essentially no weathering prior to the cutting of channels at the base of Unit 100.

1000   121.9+ cm   Alternation of sandstone and silty sandstone. Sandstone: arkosic, mottled pale yellowish-brown 10YR-6/2 and grayish orange-pink 5YR-7/2, fine- to medium-grained, clear quartz and feldspar; black mineral common as an accessory; firmly cemented, siliceous; splits massive; lenticular thin-to thick-bedded; cross-bedded, lenticular medium to low angle, small- to medium-scale trough; weathers blocky; forms irregular ledge; environment, quiet to torrential fluvial; base is sharp and irregular with 121.9 cm of relief.

Silty sandstone: olive gray 5Y-4/1 to light olive gray 5Y-5/2, clay to fine-grained sand; black mineral common as an accessory; weakly cemented, siliceous; splits shaley; flat and lenticular very thin- to thick-bedded; cross-bedded, lenticular very low angle, very large-scale; weathers hackly; forms irregular slope; alternation and metamorphosed, chiefly influx of silica that cemented the grains; environment, quiet fluvial; base is gradational and sharp.

Appendix C

ADDITIONAL CHRONOLOGICAL DATA ON CIENEGA VALLEY, ARIZONA

Bruce B. Huckell

This brief appendix is designed to integrate some additional information on the chronological interpretation of the Cienega Valley archaeology and stratigraphy. The original study by Frank W. Eddy and Maurice E. Cooley, even though more than 25 years old, remains an excellent example of an interdisciplinary approach to the study of past human adaptations to changing environmental conditions. Virtually no potential source of information that could then contribute to the investigation of the problem went unexplored. This is all the more impressive when it is realized that this effort took place relatively early in the development of interdisciplinary studies and that the work was carried out with limited funding. Despite the passing of two and a half decades, the work remains viable and useful, and provides us with the only detailed knowledge available on environmental and cultural events in the Cienega Creek Basin over the last 3,000 years.

ADDITIONAL RADIOCARBON DATES

Following a practice that had been employed in other studies of early archaeological sites (see Haury 1957; Haury, Sayles, and Wasley 1959), radiocarbon samples from Cienega Creek and Matty Wash were submitted to two different laboratories for analysis. The two laboratories chosen for the work were the University of Arizona Carbon-14 Age Determination Laboratory (now the Radiocarbon Dating Laboratory) and the Shell Development Laboratory. The Arizona facility analyzed most of the samples. At that time the Shell laboratory utilized the CO_2 gas method, while the University of Arizona employed the solid carbon method. At the time the final report manuscript was completed, only the dates provided by these laboratories using these methods were available.

In 1960 the Arizona laboratory converted to the gas method of sample analysis (Damon and Long 1962: 239), and among the early assays undertaken with this method were a few samples from Cienega Valley. Included were the samples listed in Table C.1 (see Damon and Long 1962: 245; Damon, Long, and Sigalove 1963: 293–294). These assays provide more information on the chronological aspects of the study.

The A–88 bis date is a rerun of a sample collected from the M_1 marker bed in Unit 3 (see Table 3.1). The solid carbon date of 2860 ± 210 B.P. (A–88 av.) shows more

TABLE C.1
Cienega Valley Radiocarbon Dates by the Gas Method

Sample number	Date (Years B.P.)	Context
A–88 bis	2010 ± 150	M_1 marker bed
A–92	2220 ± 150	M_2 marker bed
A–196	2190 ± 100	3E–3F boundary (top of M_2 marker bed)
A–227a	2140 ± 60	Carbonaceous earth (unit uncertain)
A–227b	1790 ± 400	Soluble fraction of A–227a

A: University of Arizona Carbon–14 Age Determination Laboratory (1958).

than 800 years difference from the gas date of 2010 ± 150 B.P. (A–88 bis). In addition, Damon and Long (1962: 245) cite a private communication indicating that the Shell laboratory also obtained a date of 1850 ± 70 B.P. (Sh–5664–7) from this same unit. Other Shell laboratory dates from the M_1 marker bed are presented in Table 3.1 and most of these are slightly younger than the Arizona gas method date. Unfortunately, the relationship of the Sh–5664–7 date cited by Damon and Long to the Sh–5664a, b, and average dates is not clear. This discrepancy between the University of Arizona solid carbon assay and the Shell laboratory gas results is noted in Chapter 3. In fact, however, the reanalysis of the Arizona date brings the determinations of the two labs much closer to agreement, and shows a significant degree of overlap in their age ranges.

The second date in Table C.1, 2220 ± 150 B.P. (A–92), comes from the M_2 marker bed within Unit 3. No samples were dated by the Arizona laboratory while using the solid carbon method, so it is not possible to directly compare the results of the two techniques in this case. The Shell facility ran two samples from the M_2 marker bed, obtaining dates of 2470 ± 200 B.P. (Sh–5665) and 2150 ± 140 B.P. (Sh–5389; see Table 3.1). Damon and Long (1962: 245) also report a date of 2470 ± 100 B.P. for Sh–5665–10, obtained from a sample collected from the same unit. How this date relates to Sh–5665, 2470 ± 200 B.P. (Table 3.1) is not known. In any case, these determinations compare closely with the Arizona date; all fall within one standard deviation of one another.

The third date presented in Table C.1, 2190 ± 100 B.P. (A–196), is described as coming from the "3E–3F boundary" (see description of section MC–5), which should place

TABLE C.2
Calibrated Radiocarbon Dates from the Cienega Valley Area

Sample Number	Date	Calibrated Date
A–74	1950 ± 200 B.P.	395 B.C.–A.D. 425
A–85	2550 ± 330 B.P.	1345 B.C.–35 B.C.
A–86a	3080 ± 300 B.P.	1945 B.C.–785 B.C.
A–86b	3660 ± 400 B.P.	2275 B.C.–1540 B.C.
A–86c	3180 ± 300 B.P.	2125 B.C.–820 B.C.
A–86 av	3300 ± 230 B.P.	2005 B.C.–1130 B.C.
A–87	2610 ± 250 B.P.	1390 B.C.–165 B.C.
A–88a	2980 ± 300 B.P.	1855 B.C.–610 B.C.
A–88b	2740 ± 250 B.P.	1560 B.C.–385 B.C.
A–88 av	2860 ± 210 B.P.	1535 B.C.–630 B.C.
A–88 bis*	2010 ± 150 B.P.	390 B.C.–A.D. 235
A–89a	3180 ± 300 B.P.	2125 B.C.–820 B.C.
A–89b	2620 ± 200 B.P.	1235 B.C.–395 B.C.
A–89c	2520 ± 300 B.P.	1265 B.C.–20 B.C.
A–89 av	2770 ± 170 B.P.	1335 B.C.–620 B.C.
A–92*	2220 ± 150 B.P.	750 B.C.–A.D. 25
A–196*	2190 ± 100 B.P.	410 B.C.–A.D. 10
A–227a*	2140 ± 60 B.P.	390 B.C.–5 B.C.
A–227b*	1790 ± 400 B.P.	170 B.C.–A.D. 625
Sh–5356*	2800 ± 190 B.P.	1410 B.C.–600 B.C.
Sh–5357*	3570 ± 210 B.P.	2520 B.C.–1555 B.C.
Sh–5358*	1850 ± 150 B.P.	165 B.C.–A.D. 440
Sh–5664a*	1940 ± 170 B.P.	370 B.C.–A.D. 345
Sh–5664b*	1760 ± 190 B.P.	160 B.C.–A.D. 600
Sh–5664 av*	1860 ± 130 B.P.	165 B.C.–A.D. 435
Sh–5664–7*	1850 ± 70 B.P.	A.D. 5–A.D. 245
Sh–5665*	2470 ± 200 B.P.	1020 B.C.–170 B.C.
Sh–5665–10*	2470 ± 100 B.P.	810 B.C.–395 B.C.
Sh–5389*	2150 ± 140 B.P.	545 B.C.–A.D. 200

*CO_2 gas method dates.
A: University of Arizona Carbon–14 Age Determination Laboratory (1957, 1958).
Sh: Shell Development Laboratory (1958).
Source of calibrated dates: Klein and others 1982.

it on the contact between the M_2 marker bed and an overlying subunit of silty sand. This date compares closely with dates from the M_2 marker bed itself, as may be seen in Table 3.1.

The final two dates were obtained on two fractions of carbonaceous earth, apparently collected as part of Paul Martin's alluvial pollen research in southeastern Arizona (see Martin 1963): 2140 ± 60 B.P. (A–227a) and 1790 ± 400 B.P. (A–227b). The sample was not tied into the stratigraphic framework developed by Cooley, though it would appear to fall in the older portion of the Unit 3 time range.

The primary value of these additional dates is that they provide a means of evaluating the earlier radiocarbon determinations. Clearly there is a high level of agreement between the CO_2 method dates performed by both the Shell laboratory and the University of Arizona laboratory. It is unfortunate that more of the old solid carbon assays were not reanalyzed using the gas method so that their accuracy could be directly assessed. The gas method has replaced the solid carbon method because it gives better results, so it is probable that the gas method dates are the more accurate ones in this case. Thus, the solid carbon dates shown in Table 3.1 are likely to be somewhat less reflective of the true age of the archaeological features and stratigraphic units from which the samples were collected.

CALIBRATION OF CIENEGA VALLEY RADIOCARBON DATES

The conversion of radiocarbon dates in the years before present to Christian calendric dates has recently been intensively studied. The calibration of radiocarbon dates must take into account temporal variations in the natural radiocarbon content of the atmospheric carbon dioxide, and a recently published study (Klein and others 1982) provides the most up-to-date calibration available. Resulting from a comprehensive study of the results of radiocarbon activity measurements on over 1100 samples of dendrochronologically dated wood at five separate laboratories, this calibration permits a confidence level of 95 percent in the conversion of a radiocarbon date to a calendric date. Table C.2 presents the Cienega Valley dates converted by using the tables presented by Klein and others (1982: 124–150). The reader is referred to that publication for an explanation of the generation of the calibration tables and the methods for their use. The dates shown in Table C.2 include both the earlier Arizona laboratory solid carbon determinations and the later Arizona and Shell laboratory CO_2 gas dates.

It is hoped that the information presented in this appendix will add to the value and utility of Eddy and Cooley's study, and assist in further chronological interpretations of the prehistory of this important area.

REFERENCES

Antevs, Ernst
1955 Geologic-climatic dating in the West. *American Antiquity* 20(4): 317-335.

Barghoorn, Elso S., Margaret K. Wolfe, and Kathryn H. Clisby
1954 Fossil maize from the Valley of Mexico. *Botanical Museum Leaflets, Harvard University*, 16(9): 229-240.

Bartlett, John Russell
1854 *Personal Narrative of Explorations and Incidents in Texas, New Mexico, California, Sonora, and Chihuahua, Connected with the United States and Mexican Boundary Commission During the Years 1850, '51, '52, and '53.* 2 vols. New York: Appleton.

Bryan, Kirk
1925 Date of channel trenching in the arid Southwest. *Science* 62(1607): 338-344.
1940 Erosion in the valleys of the Southwest. *New Mexico Quarterly* 10(4): 227-232.

Bryson, Reid A.
1957 The annual march of precipitation in Arizona, New Mexico and Northwestern Mexico. *University of Arizona, Technical Reports on the Meterology and Climatology of Arid Regions* 6. Tucson: University of Arizona.

Colton, Harold S.
1955 Pottery types of the Southwest: Wares 8A, 8B, 9A, 9B, Tusayan Gray, and White Ware. *Museum of Northern Arizona Ceramic Series* 3. Flagstaff: Museum of Northern Arizona.

Cooley, Maurice E.
1958 Recent alluvial geology of Cienega Valley in the area at the confluence of Matty Wash with Cienega Creek, Pima County, Arizona. In "A Sequence of Cultural and Alluvial Deposits in the Cienega Creek Basin, Southeastern Arizona" by Frank W. Eddy, Appendix A. MS, master's thesis, Department of Anthropology, University of Arizona, Tucson.

Damon, Paul E., and Austin Long
1962 Arizona Radiocarbon Dates III. *Radiocarbon* 4: 239-249.

Damon, Paul E., Austin Long, and Joel E. Sigalove
1963 Arizona Radiocarbon Dates IV. *Radiocarbon* 5: 283-301.

Damon, Paul E., Austin Long, and E. Wallick
1972 *Dendrochronologic calibration of the carbon-14 time scale.* Contribution 57, Department of Geosciences, University of Arizona; contribution to the 8th International Radiocarbon Dating Conference, New Zealand.

Danson, Edward B.
1957a Pottery type descriptions. Appendix G in "Excavations, 1940 at University Indian Ruin, Tucson, Arizona" by Julian D. Hayden. *Southwestern Monuments Association, Technical Series* 5. Globe: Southwestern Monuments Association.
1957b Trait list: Tucson phase. Appendix H in "Excavations, 1940 at University Indian Ruin, Tucson, Arizona" by Julian D. Hayden. *Southwestern Monuments Association, Technical Series* 5. Globe: Southwestern Monuments Association.

Deevey, E. S., and R. F. Flint
1957 Postglacial hypsithermal interval. *Science* 125(3240): 182-184.

Di Peso, Charles C.
1951 The Babocomari Village Site on the Babocomari River, southeastern Arizona. *The Amerind Foundation* 5. Dragoon, Arizona: Amerind Foundation.
1953 The Sobaipuri Indians of the upper San Pedro River Valley, southeastern Arizona. *The Amerind Foundation* 6. Dragoon, Arizona: Amerind Foundation.
1956 The Upper Pima of San Cayetano del Tumacacori: an archaeohistorical reconstruction of the Ootam of Pimeria Alta. *The Amerind Foundation* 7. Dragoon, Arizona: Amerind Foundation.

Drake, Robert J.
1958a Nonmarine molluscan remains from Recent sediments in Matty Canyon, Pima County, Arizona. Appendix D in "A Sequence of Cultural and Alluvial Deposits in the Cienega Creek Basin, Southeastern Arizona," by Frank W. Eddy. MS, master's thesis, Department of Anthropology, University of Arizona, Tucson.
1958b Nonmarine molluscan remains from Recent sediments in Matty Canyon, Pima County, Arizona. *Bulletin of the Southern California Academy of Sciences* 58(3): 146-154.

Eddy, Frank W.
1958 A Sequence of Cultural and Alluvial Deposits in the Cienega Creek Basin, Southeastern Arizona. MS, master's thesis, Department of Anthropology, University of Arizona, Tucson.

Faegri, Knut, and Johs. Iversen
1950 *Text-Book of Modern Pollen Analysis.* Copenhagen: Ejnar Munksgaard.

Gladwin, Harold S., Emil W. Haury, E. B. Sayles, and Nora Gladwin
1937 Excavations at Snaketown: Material Culture. *Medallion Papers* 25. Globe, Arizona: Gila Pueblo.

Hack, John T.
1942 The Changing Physical Environment of the Hopi Indians of Arizona. *Papers of the Peabody Museum, Harvard University*, 35(1).

Haury, Emil W.
1943 A possible Cochise-Mogollon-Hohokam sequence. *Proceedings of the American Philosophical Society* 86(2): 260-263.
1950 *The Stratigraphy and Archaeology of Ventana Cave, Arizona.* Tucson: University of Arizona Press and Albuquerque: University of New Mexico Press.
1957 An alluvial site on the San Carlos Indian Reservation, Arizona. *American Antiquity* 23(1): 2-27.
1976 *The Hohokam. Desert Farmers and Craftsmen.* Tucson: University of Arizona Press.

Haury, Emil W., E. B. Sayles, and William W. Wasley
1959 The Lehner mammoth site, southeastern Arizona. *American Antiquity* 25(1): 2-30.

Hayden, Julian D.
1957 Excavations, 1940 at University Indian Ruin, Tucson, Arizona. *Southwestern Monuments Association Technical Series* 5. Globe, Arizona: Southwestern Monuments Association.

Jennings, Jesse D.
1957 Danger Cave. *Memoirs of the Society for American Archaeology* 14.

Johnson, Frederick
1951 Radiocarbon dating: a report on the program to aid in the development of the method of dating. *Memoirs of the Society for American Archaeology* 8.

Kelly, Isabel
1938 Hodges Site Materials. MS on file in the Arizona State Museum Library, University of Arizona, Tucson.
1978 The Hodges Ruin: A Hohokam Community in the Tucson Basin. *Anthropological Papers of the University of Arizona* 30. Tucson: University of Arizona Press.

Klein, Jeffrey, J. C. Lerman, Paul E. Damon, and E. K. Ralph
1982 Calibration of radiocarbon dates: tables based on the consensus data of the Workshop on Calibrating the Radiocarbon Time Scale. *Radiocarbon* 24(2): 103-150.

McGregor, John C.
1941 *Southwestern Archaeology*. New York: John Wiley.

Marshall, Joe T., Jr.
1957 Birds of Pine-Oak Woodland in southern Arizona and adjacent Mexico. *Pacific Coast Avifauna* 32. Berkeley: Cooper Ornithological Society.

Martin, Paul Schultz
1963 *The Last 10,000 Years: A Fossil Pollen Record of the American Southwest*. Tucson: University of Arizona Press.

Martin, Paul Schultz, James Schoenwetter, and Bernard C. Arms
1961 *The Last 10,000 Years: Southwest Palynology and Prehistory*. Tucson: Geochronology Laboratories, University of Arizona.

Opler, Morris E.
1941 *An Apache Life-Way: The Economic, Social, and Religious Institutions of the Chiricahua Indians*. Chicago: University of Chicago Press.

Pomeroy, J. Anthony
1959 Hohokam etched shell. *The Kiva* 25(4): 12-20.

Sayles, E. B.
1945 The San Simon Branch. Excavations at Cave Creek and in the San Simon Valley. Material Culture. *Medallion Papers* 34. Globe, Arizona: Gila Pueblo.
1983 The Cochise Cultural Sequence in Southeastern Arizona. *Anthropological Papers of the University of Arizona* 42. Tucson: University of Arizona Press.

Sayles, E. B., and Ernest Antevs
1941 The Cochise Culture. *Medallion Papers* 29. Globe, Arizona: Gila Pueblo.

Schoenwetter, James
1960 Pollen Analysis of Sediments from Matty Wash. MS, master's thesis, Department of Anthropology, University of Arizona, Tucson.

Sellers, William D., editor
1960 *Arizona Climate*. Tucson: Institute of Atmospheric Physics, University of Arizona.

Shreve, Forrest
1939 Observations on the vegetation of Chihuahua. *Madrono* 5: 1-13. Berkeley: California Botanical Society.

Shutler, Dick, Jr., and Paul E. Damon
1959 University of Arizona radiocarbon dates II. *American Journal of Science, Radiocarbon Supplement* 1: 59-62.

Smith, H. V.
1956 The Climate of Arizona. *Agricultural Experiment Station, Bulletin* 279. Tucson: University of Arizona.

Steward, Julian H.
1955 *Theory of Culture Change: The Methodology of Multilinear Evolution*. Urbana: University of Illinois Press.

Swanson, Earl H., Jr.
1951 An Archaeological Survey of the Empire Valley, Arizona. MS, master's thesis, Department of Anthropology, University of Arizona, Tucson.

Thomas, Harold E.
1963 General summary of effects of the drought in the southwest, 1942-56. *United States Geological Survey, Professional Paper* 372-H. Washington.

Trewartha, Glenn T.
1953 Climates of the earth. In *Goode's World Atlas*, edited by Edward B. Espenshade, Jr., 9th edition, pp. 8-9. Chicago: Rand McNally.

Trischka, Carl
1933 Hohokam: a chapter in the history of red-on-buff culture of Arizona. *Scientific Monthly* 37(5): 417-433.

Tuthill, Carr
1947 The Tres Alamos Site on the San Pedro River, southeastern Arizona. *The Amerind Foundation* 4. Dragoon, Arizona: Amerind Foundation.

Wasley, William W.
1957 *The Archaeological Survey of the Arizona State Museum*. Tucson: Arizona State Museum.

Wheat, Joe Ben
1955 Mogollon culture prior to A.D. 1000. *Memoirs of the Society for American Archaeology* 10.

Wise, E. N., and Dick Shutler, Jr.
1958 University of Arizona radiocarbon dates. *Science* 127(3289): 72-74.

INDEX

Agriculture, incipient, 23, 47–50. *See also* Corn; Subsistence economy
Alluvium. *See* Recent alluvium
Altithermal, 46; Fig. 2.16
Anathermal, Fig. 2.16
Antevs, Ernst, vii
Archaic tradition, vii
Architecture. *See* Jacal structures; Pit houses
Arizona Carbon-14 Age Determination Laboratory, ix, 31, 57. *See also* Radiocarbon dating
Arizona EE:2:10, ix, 9, 11, 22–24; Figs. 1.3, 2.7
Arizona EE:2:11, 26; Fig. 1.3
Arizona EE:2:12, 10; Fig. 1.3
Arizona EE:2:14, 12, 25
Arizona EE:2:30, ix, 10, 17–23, 32, 44, 46–47; Fig. 1.3, Table 2.1
Arizona EE:2:34, ix, 25–26; Figs. 1.3, 2.8, 2.14
Arizona EE:2:35, ix, 10, 32, 44; Fig. 1.3, Tables 2.1, 3.1
Arizona EE:2:36, 12; Fig. 1.3
Arizona EE:2:38, 15–17
Arizona EE:2:40, 24; Fig. 1.3
Arizona EE:2:41, 15
Airzona EE:2:42, 25
Arizona EE:2:45, 27
Arizona Pioneers Historical Society, 33
Arizona State Museum, 23
Arroyo cutting, 1, 9, 40
Awls. *See* Bone tools

Barnett, Fred, x, 6, 15
Barnett, Harry, x
Base camp, San Pedro stage, 17
Benson 5:10, 17, 32; Fig. 1.1
Bone tools, 22
 awls, 22; Fig. 2.13
 cylinder, 22; Fig. 2.13
 flakers, 22; Fig. 2.13
 hammer, 22; Fig. 2.13
 tube, 22
Burial pits. *See* Burials, inhumations
Burials
 cremations, 11–12
 inhumations, 17, 22–23
  dog, 23; Fig. 2.3
  human, 12, 22–23, 46

Cañada del Oro phase. *See* Hohokam culture

Cañada del Oro-Rillito phase. *See* Hohokam culture
Ceramic dating, 32–33; Table 2.4
Ceramic sites, 10–15
 buried pit houses, 10–11; Figs. 2.7, 2.8
 buried trash zones, 11–12
 ridge sites, 15
 sheet erosion sites, 12–15
Ceramic types, Table 2.4
 Babocomari Polychrome, 27
 Estrella Grooved, 24
 Gila Butte Red-on-buff, 25
 Gila Polychrome, 27
 Mimbres Black-on-white, 27
 Rincon Plain, 26; Fig. 2.15
 Rincon Red-on-brown, 12, 26; Fig. 2.15
 Roosevelt Black-on-white, 27
 Santa Cruz Polychrome, 27
 Santa Cruz Red-on-brown series, 30
 Snaketown Grooved, 24
 Tanque Verde Red-on-brown, 15, 26–27
 Vahki plain and red, 23
Chipped stone tools, 21; Table 2.3
 disk, 21; Fig. 2.12
 planes, 21; Fig. 2.12
 projectile points, 10; Figs. 2.1, 2.12
 scrapers, 10, 21; Figs. 2.1, 2.12
 waste chips, 21
Chiricahua stage. *See* Cochise culture
Cienega Creek, 1; Fig. 1.3
Cienega Ranch, x; Fig. 1.3
Cienegas, 1, 6, 35, 42, 45
Cienega Valley, 1; Figs. 1.2, 1.5, 1.6
Climate, 2–4; Table 1.1, Fig. 4.2
Clovis hunters, vii; Fig. 2.16
Cochise culture, vii, ix, 1, 17–23; Fig. 2.16
 Chiricahua stage, vii
 San Pedro stage, vii, 1, 17, 46–47
 Sulphur Spring stage, vii
Cockrum, E. Lendell, x
Comin's Fellowship Fund, ix
Cooking pits. *See* Pits
Cooley, Maurice E., x, 57
Corn, 42–43, 46. *See also* Pollen profiles; Subsistence economy
Cremations. *See* Burials
Cretaceous rocks, 6
 Unit 1000, Fig. 2.16, Appendix B
Cruciform object. *See* Ground stone tools
Cummings, Byron, vii, ix
Cylinder. *See* Bone tools

Danson, Edward B., ix
Dating. *See* Ceramic dating; Radiocarbon dating
Debitage. *See* Chipped stone tools, waste chips
Desert culture, 27
Disks. *See* Chipped stone tools; Ground stone tools
Dog burial, 23; Fig. 2.3
Drake, Robert J., x

Eddy, Frank, x, 17, 57
Empire mountains, 1; Fig. 1.1
Empire Ranch, ix, 33; Fig. 1.1
Empire Valley, ix, 1; Fig. 1.1, 1.4
Enzenberg, Orion, 6

Falls, Lower and Upper, Figs. 1.3, 5.1
Ferguson, C. Wes, x
Fire hearths. *See* Hearths
Flakers. *See* Bone tools
Folsom hunters, vii
Folsom, New Mexico, vii

Gastropods. *See* Invertebrates
Gathering. *See* Subsistence economy
Geological sections, ix; Figs. 1.3, 5.1
 MC-1, 8, 36, 45; Table 3.2
 MC-2, Fig. 5.1
 MC-3, Figs. 1.6, 5.1
 MC-4, 36
 MC-5, ix, 2, 10, 34, 42, 45–47; Fig. 1.6, Appendix A
 MC-6, ix, 42, 45–47; Figs. 1.5, 1.6, Appendix B
 MC-7, 15, 32, 40
Gila Pueblo, 23
Gravel surface "S," 25; Figs. 2.8, 2.14
Great Drought, 50; Fig. 2.16
Greenway, J. S., x
Ground stone tools, 18; Table 2.3
 cruciform object, 19
 disks, 19; Fig. 2.11
 handstones, 18; Fig. 2.10
 mano, 27
 metate, 27
 millingstones, 19; Fig. 2.1
 pebble hammerstones, 18; Fig. 2.11
 pecking stone, 18; Fig. 2.11
 protopestle, 19; Fig. 2.10
 slab grinding stone, 18; Fig. 2.11
 trapezoidal objects, 19; Fig. 2.12

Hammers. *See* Bone tools; Ground stone tools, pebble hammerstones
Handstones. *See* Ground stone tools
Haury, Emil W., ix, x, 12, 17
Hearths, 10, 17, 18, 23–25, 32. *See also* Pits, cooking
Hester, James J., x; Table 2.2
Hilton, E., 6
Historic remains, 15
Hodges Ruin, 23
Hohokam culture, vii, 1, 23, 26–30; Fig. 2.16
    Cañada del Oro phase, 25
    Cañada del Oro–Rillito phase, 11, 25
    Rincon phase, 26–27
    Snaketown phase, 24
    Tanque Verde phase, 12, 27, 50
    Tucson phase, 27, 50
    Vahki–Estrella phase, 10, 23–24
Hohokam periods, Fig. 2.16
    Classic, 47–50
    Colonial, 47
    Pioneer, 11, 47
    Sedentary, 47, 50
Humphrey, Robert R., ix
Hunting. *See* Subsistence economy

Inhumations. *See* Burials
Invertebrates (gastropods), 44; Table 4.1

Jacal structures, 26, 30

Maize. *See* Pollen profiles; Subsistence economy
Mammal bone indentifications, 44, Table 2.2
Mano. *See* Ground stone tools
Marker beds, Figs. 1.6, 2.16, 5.1
    K–marker bed, 9, 12, 47
    M–marker beds, 32, 34, 46, 57; Table C.1
    X–marker bed, 9, 12
Martin, Paul, ix, 5, 42–44
Matty Canyon, ix
Matty Wash, 1; Fig. 1.3
Measured geological sections. *See* Geological sections
Medithermal, Fig. 2.16
Metate. *See* Ground stone tools

Millingstones. *See* Ground stone tools
Mogollon culture, vii, 26–30

Neothermal period, Fig. 2.16
    Altithermal, 46; Fig. 2.16
    Anathermal, Fig. 2.16
    Medithermal, Fig. 2.16

Paleo–Indians, vii; Fig. 2.16
Pecking stone. *See* Ground stone tools
Peppersauce Wash, 32; Fig. 1.1
Physiography, 1–2
Pit houses, 10–11, 17, 23–30, 46, 47; Figs. 2.4, 2.7, 2.8, 2.14
Pits
    burial, 17. *See also* Burials
    cooking, 17, 44, 46; Figs. 2.6, 2.9
    storage, 17
Planes. *See* Chipped stone tools
Plants. *See* Pollen profiles; Vegetation
Pleistocene deposits, 6–7; Fig. 2.16
    Unit 100, 33
Pollen profiles, 42–44; Figs. 2.16, 4.3
    chenopod-amaranths, 42
    composites, 45
    cyperaceae, 45
    maize (*Zea mays*; corn), 42–43, 46
    mesquite, 42
    oak, 42, 45
    pine, 42, 45
    teosinte, 42
    See also Vegetation
Pottery. *See* Ceramic types
Preceramic sites, 10
Projectile points. *See* Chipped stone tools
Protopestle. *See* Ground stone tools

Radiocarbon dating, 31–32; Table 3.1, Appendix C
    calibration, 31, 58; Table C.2
    gas (CO_2) method, 31, 57
    solid carbon method, 31, 57
Recent alluvium, 7–9; Figs. 1.6, 2.16, 4.1
    Unit 1, 9, 34
    Unit 2 (Sanford formation), 7, 9, 12, 34, 37–40, 50
    Unit 3, 9, 34, 40–42
    Unit 4, 8, 34, 40–42
    Unit 5, 8, 33
    Unit 6, 8, 33
    Unit 7, 7, 32–33
Rincon phase. *See* Hohokam culture

Salado culture, 27
Sanford formation. *See* Recent alluvium, Unit 2
Sanford Ranch, 15, 33; Fig. 1.3
San Pedro stage. *See* Cochise culture
Sayles, E. B., vii, x
Schaldach, W. J., Jr., x, Table 2.2
Schoenwetter, James, ix
Scrapers. *See* Chipped stone tools
Shell Development Laboratory, ix, 31, 57; Appendix C
    See also Radiocarbon dating
Shell ornaments, 27
Shoshonean Indians, 23
Slab grinding stone. *See* Ground stone tools
Smiley, Terah L., x
Snaketown phase. *See* Hohokam culture
Snaketown site, 32
Storage pits. *See* Pits
Subsistence economy, 21–30, 46–50
Sulphur Spring stage. *See* Cochise culture
Swanson, Earl H., ix

Tanque Verde phase. *See* Hohokam culture
Trapezoidal objects. *See* Ground stone tools
Tres Alamos site, 23; Fig. 1.1
Tube. *See* Bone tools
Tucson phase. *See* Hohokam culture
Tularosa Cave, 32

Waste chips. *See* Chipped stone tools
Whetstone mountains, 1; Fig. 1.1
Whitewater Draw, vii
Wildlife, 5–6
Wood identifications, 44; Table 2.1
Wright, R. A., x

Vail, Walter, 33
Vegetation, 4–5, 47; Table 1.2, Fig. 1.4
    See also Pollen profiles; Subsistence economy
Ventana Cave, 33, 46; Table 2.3